AF575477

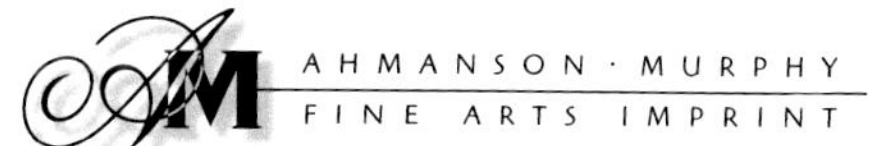

THE AHMANSON FOUNDATION
has endowed this imprint
to honor the memory of
FRANKLIN D. MURPHY
who for half a century
served arts and letters,
beauty and learning, in
equal measure by shaping
with a brilliant devotion
those institutions upon
which they rely.

The publisher gratefully acknowledges the generous contribution to this book provided by the Graham Foundation for Advanced Studies in the Fine Arts.

The publisher also gratefully acknowledges the generous support of the Art Endowment Fund of the University of California Press Foundation, which was established by a major gift from the Ahmanson Foundation, and of the Richard and Harriett Gold Endowment Fund in Arts and Humanities of the University of California Press Foundation.

SCHINDLER, KINGS ROAD,
AND SOUTHERN CALIFORNIA MODERNISM

SCHINDLER, KINGS ROAD, AND SOUTHERN CALIFORNIA MODERNISM

ROBERT SWEENEY
JUDITH SHEINE

INTRODUCTION BY MARK MACK
PHOTOGRAPHY BY TIMOTHY SAKAMOTO

UNIVERSITY OF CALIFORNIA PRESS
In association with Friends of the Schindler House

University of California Press, one of the most distinguished university presses in the United States, enriches lives around the world by advancing scholarship in the humanities, social sciences, and natural sciences. Its activities are supported by the UC Press Foundation and by philanthropic contributions from individuals and institutions. For more information, visit www.ucpress.edu.

University of California Press
Oakland, California

LIBRARY OF CONGRESS CATALOGING-IN-PUBLICATION DATA

Sweeney, Robert L. (Robert Lawrence), 1945– author.
Schindler, Kings Road, and southern California modernism / Robert Sweeney, Judith Sheine ; introduction by Mark Mack ; photography by Timothy Sakamoto. — 1st [edition].
pages cm
Includes bibliographical references and index.
ISBN 978-0-520-27194-4 (cloth : alk. paper)
1. Schindler, R. M. (Rudolph M.), 1887–1953—Criticism and interpretation. 2. Schindler House (Los Angeles, Calif.) 3. Schindler, R. M. (Rudolph M.), 1887–1953—Homes and haunts. 4. West Hollywood (Calif.)—Buildings, structures, etc. 5. Modern movement (Architecture)—California, Southern. I. Sheine, Judith, author. II. Sakamoto, Timothy, illustrator. III. Title.
NA7238.L6S94 2012
720.92—dc23 2012006830
GPSR Authorized Representative: Easy Access System Europe, Mustamäe tee 50, 10621 Tallinn, Estonia, gpsr.requests@easproject.com

30 29 28 27 26
10 9 8 7 6 5

The paper used in this publication meets the minimum requirements of ANSI/NISO Z39.48–1992 (R 2002) (*Permanence of Paper*).

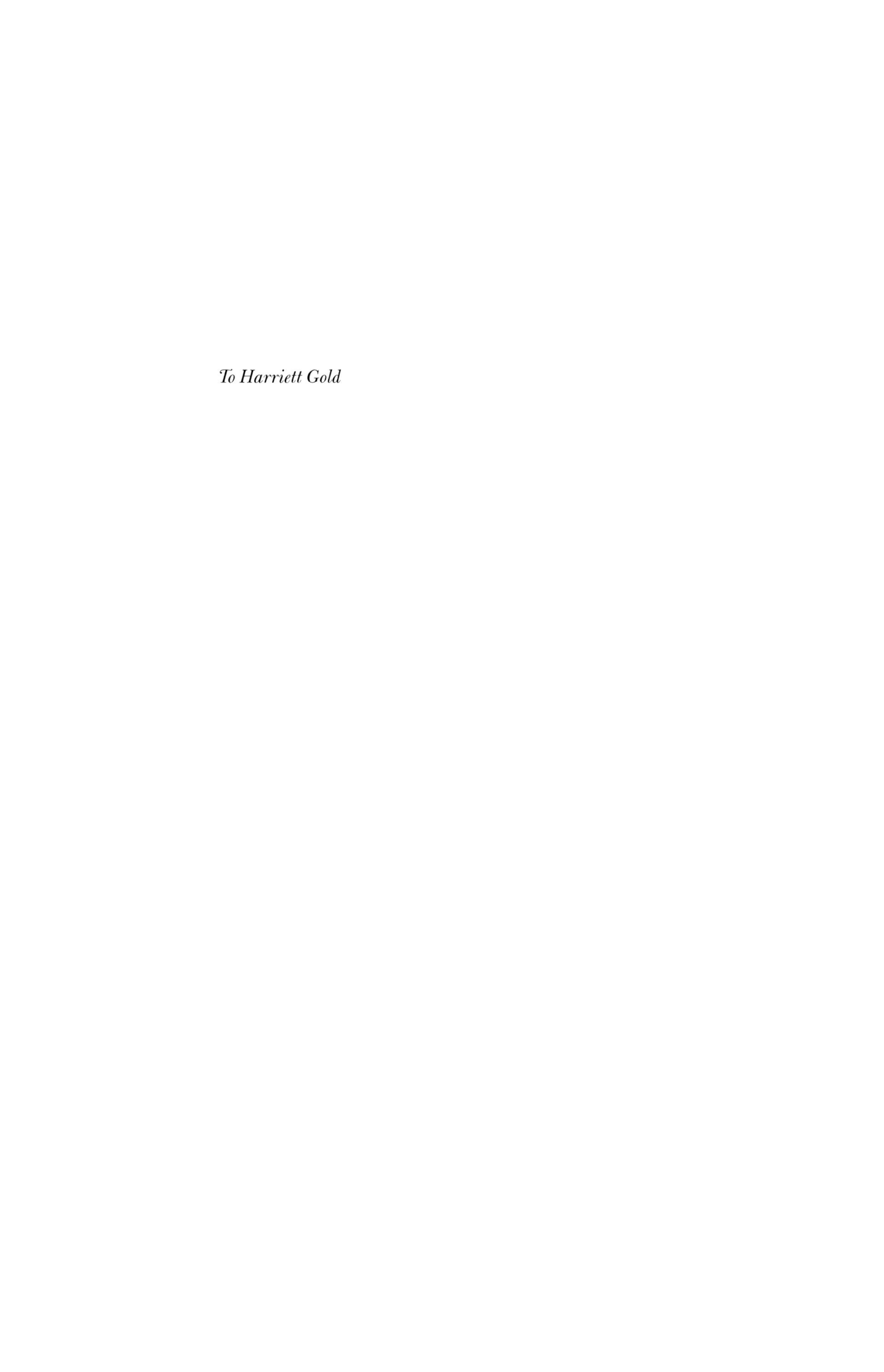

To Harriett Gold

CONTENTS

ACKNOWLEDGMENTS

THE MANUSCRIPT for this book was developed in two distinct phases. It began in 2000 in a different guise entirely when Daniela Zyman, then chief curator at the Österreichisches Museum für Angewandte Kunst (Austrian Museum of Applied Arts), Vienna, asked me to prepare an essay on Schindler's influences. With the generous consent of Peter Noever, I spent the month of October 2000 in Vienna as a guest of the MAK, following Schindler's trail and assembling a detailed body of information about his education and associations there. I was very fortunate to have Christine Schwaiger working with me. Christine not only kept up, she anticipated. Along the way we crossed paths with Peter Bojčzuk, Otto Antonia Graf, Hans Hollein, Markus Kristan, Friedrich Kurrent, August Sarnitz, and Johannes Spalt; all are thanked. I made a brief detour to Prague in search of information about Schindler's father; Honja Skoda was my guide there. Later, on a subsequent trip to Vienna, Christiane Irxenmayer helped assemble illustrations. Ultimately the publication Daniela Zyman envisioned was abandoned for reasons unrelated to my involvement.

The Vienna material sat dormant for a decade until the decision was reached to produce a new book on Schindler's Kings Road house. Judith Sheine has joined me in this undertaking; we owe an extraordinary debt to Harriett Gold and Deborah Kirshman for encouraging the University of California Press to take it on. John Mason Caldwell did what was necessary to complete the package.

Research on Schindler has been a passion of many years for Judith and me. I focused on Kings Road, while Judith looked at the larger picture—a chemistry that determined the format of this book. Along the way, Mark Schindler (1922–2012), Mary Schindler, and Anne Harriet Chace Eastwood responded repeatedly to requests for information. Schindler clients and homeowners Adolph Tischler, Jacqueline and William Sharlin, and Michael LaFetra were, as ever, generous in allowing us to photograph their houses. We also appreciate Jonathan Richert and Jeffrey Blitz, as well as staff at the MAK Center at the

Schindler House, for their assistance in photographing the Kings Road house. Matt Walla provided crucial technical assistance in reproducing vintage illustration material; and Tim Lanza, Douris UK Ltd., and John Bengtson helped with access to the image from Buster Keaton's 1924 film *Sherlock, Jr.* Jocelyn Gibbs and Alex Hauschild provided welcome breaths of fresh air at the Architecture and Design Collection, Art, Design & Architecture Museum, University of California, Santa Barbara. Omar Velazquez and Isrrael Fuentes undertook the most ambitious work in the garden since restoration was completed in 1989. As the photographs show, it has never looked finer.

Lionel March and Lauren Weiss Bricker offered thoughtful comments on Judith Sheine's draft essay, and Susan Jacobs Lockhart and Benny Chan were generous in allowing the use of their photographs. Most of all, we would like to thank Tim Sakamoto, whose new photographs of Kings Road will, for many, supply the lasting impression of this book.

Staff at the University of California Press—especially Kari Dahlgren, Eric Schmidt, and Jacqueline Volin—guided us at once expertly and cordially in the process of seeing this book to completion. Finally, we gratefully acknowledge the help of Margaret Crawford and Jonathan Lipman with the application to the Graham Foundation, whose support made publication possible.

Robert Sweeney
with Judith Sheine

INTRODUCTION

MARK MACK

IMAGINE an architectural space that inspires an engaged discussion of radical cultural and social issues. Imagine a place where fundamental architectural ideas are crafted in a novel way, through the honest use of materials and a new programmatic order of living that conspire to envelop and seduce a new generation of southern Californians.[1] Imagine a place where we would find a collection of seminal local and international figures—the equivalents of the rapper Snoop Dogg, the blogger Arianna Huffington, the liberal actor Sean Penn, the minimalist composer John Adams, the extreme choreographer Pina Bausch, the pop photographer David LaChapelle, the even more poppy singer Madonna, the elusive artist Banksy, the successful Julian Schnabel, the sinister David Lynch, and the acerbic Mike Davis—all meeting regularly to exchange exciting ideas about social and cultural radicalism, a place where contemporary performances mix with the bohemian urge to have a good time.

Such a place did exist, from 1922 through the 1970s, at the address 835 North Kings Road in West Hollywood, California, where many of the countercultural figures of that time would go to perform, give readings, dance expressively, and vividly discuss social injustice and artistic liberties. The space allowed for the nuanced mingling of architectural sensations and the communal interactions of a variety of personalities, from political activists to actors and artists to businessmen. The influential health guru Philip Lovell, the actors Arthur Rankin and George O'Hara, the newly arrived Austrian architect Richard Neutra and family, and the already eminent Edward Weston and his entourage from Northern California were regular guests at various parties and salons. The art agent Galka Scheyer, representing Lyonel Feininger and Wassily Kandinsky; an emergent John Cage, studying with the established Arnold Schoenberg; and the eccentric bon vivant Sadakichi Hartmann all gathered in the landscaped courtyards, illuminated only by the intense glow of the outdoor fireplaces, around a modern interpretation of Balinese almost-nude dancing by the expressive dancer John Bovingdon.

It seemed that the cultural and countercultural elite were walking in and out of the three-sided rooms, which always left space for the outside to come in. It was a place where the bedrooms had no walls, where the outdoor fireplaces enhanced a campfire camaraderie, where the literal openness of the building plan demolished any established hierarchy of residential pretension.[2]

This house was and is for me one of a few architectural examples in which radical space design and its occupancy overlap in reinforcing a social and artistic dimension larger than the singularity of a modern landmark building. Perched between speculative real estate developments, the house still fights back today as a pesky neighbor upholding its values as a place where, thanks first to the initiative of Friends of the Schindler House, stewards of the building since 1980, and later to the Austrian government's sponsorship, cultural exchange reminiscent of those fantastic days of yore is still possible.[3]

This house not only represents an architectural experiment of space and flow, of seamless inside and outside transitions; as an early prototype of California living, it celebrates a history of extraordinary people floating through and residing within. It is not only, like so many architect-built houses, a concise blueprint of an architectural vision; it is also the result of a negotiated collaboration between the socially conscious community activist Pauline Gibling Schindler and her husband, reflecting their optimism about social change in a new part of the world. Away from an exploitative and capitalistic reality, they created an environment of joy, hope, and serious intellectual exchange, the new beginnings of a humanistic wonderland.

No wonder that this combination of Bolshevik humanism and spatial looseness was too much for the uptight East Coast shopkeepers of Modernism and the hawkers of the International Style—curators Henry-Russell Hitchcock, Philip Johnson, and Arthur Drexler—who chose to exclude the house from their various exhibitions on sanctified Modernism in America. It is therefore even more satisfactory to find the house now revered and appreciated for what it represents, projecting a classless and liberated social arrangement of rooms in a natural landscape, where rooms have no labels, like "bedroom" or "living room," instead only noting the occupant, the human, and his or her relationship of goodwill with others sharing that world. And it is not by coincidence that the appreciation for the house at 835 North Kings Road reemerged when similar notions of an optimistic societal drift appeared in the late 1960s, again supporting a more open and liberated climate of design, simultaneously with the emergence of radical architecture groups such as Archigram, Superstudio, and Ant Farm, whose members took some of the earliest pilgrimages to the Schindler House.

The Schindler House, as it is known, embodies for me the rare confluence of zeitgeist and timelessness, where aesthetic purity and radical politics were allowed to mingle freely. In a time such as ours today, where ideals are giving way to pragmatism and conformity, where artificial and speculative smoothness overcomes rugged individual expression, the Kings Road house, and the life lived within it, remain a lively marker of a history whose time is sorely needed again.

Architecturally I am satisfied—it is a thoroughbred—and will either attract people—or repulse them—my fate is settled—one way or other—

R. M. Schindler to Pauline G. Schindler, April 24, 1922

[I am] grateful to you, r.m.s . . . for . . . this house, which has been so dear to me that in a way it has determined life.

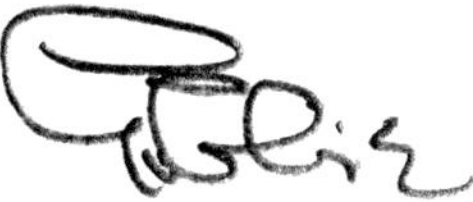

Pauline G. Schindler to R. M. Schindler, July 9, 1953

PRÉCIS

TODAY, R.M. Schindler's Kings Road house is celebrated as an icon of early Modern architecture. This wasn't always the case. Although Schindler and his wife, Pauline, recognized its genius early on, its radical appearance was—and remains—incomprehensible to many. Unlike Schindler's other seminal works of the 1920s, the Lovell Beach House and Pueblo Ribera Court, which were published in the mainstream architectural press soon after completion, Kings Road remained in the shadows. Richard Neutra looked away in his book *Wie Baut Amerika?*—written while he was living in the house with Schindler and published in 1927. And Philip Johnson, who could have legitimized the house early on, was dismissive after a visit in the early 1930s.[1]

The house finally was published—and got a nod of East Coast recognition—in 1932, in an article Schindler wrote for *T-Square,* a Philadelphia architectural journal. In discussing the innovative construction system, the integration of indoors and out, and the revisionist lifestyle embodied in the scheme, he established a basis of interpretation that has gone unchallenged for eight decades. With the exception of an unsigned article in the *Los Angeles Times* in 1953, the house was not published again in Schindler's lifetime.[2]

The situation began to change in 1960 with the appearance of *Five California Architects* by Esther McCoy, though the illustrations showed the house in a greatly altered and therefore misleading state.[3] The real explosion of interest occurred after 1980, when the house was acquired by a nonprofit organization, Friends of the Schindler House, and opened to the public. Still, the interpretation established by Schindler in 1932 continued to be accepted.

What Schindler did not provide was theoretical analysis of the design. This was outlined in his manifesto of circa 1912, "Modern Architecture: A Program," in which he proposed radical advances on the ideas of Otto Wagner, Adolf Loos, and Frank Lloyd Wright. The Kings Road house was the first manifestation of these ideas, exemplifying an architecture of "space, climate, light and mood." Similarly, it stood in contrast to Wright's contemporary

California work. Late in life, Schindler criticized Wright's buildings on Olive Hill (now Barnsdall Park in Hollywood) that "clung to the classical Greek vocabulary (base, shaft, cornice), at the same time trying to give themselves local roots by the introduction of Mayan motifs."[4]

There was another critical influence on Kings Road that has been little discussed. To an extraordinary degree, the house was a collaborative effort between Schindler and his wife, Pauline. Correspondence that became available relatively recently confirms her role in formulating the lifestyle. Writing in 1916 to her mother from Jane Addams's Hull-House, where she was working, she described the house she hoped to build:

> One of my dreams, Mother, is to have, some day, a little joy of a bungalow, on the edge of woods and mountains and near a crowded city, which shall be open just as some people's hearts are open, to friends of all classes and types. I should like it to be as democratic a meeting-place as Hull-House, where millionaires and laborers, professors and illiterates, the splendid and the ignoble meet constantly together.[5]

Clearly embracing the overall concept, Schindler gave brilliant architectural form to her social theories. Later, it was largely Mrs. Schindler's initiative that established the house as a mecca for avant-garde cultural and left-wing political activity in Los Angeles.

There is nothing comparable to Kings Road in Schindler's work, though he identified it as the point of departure for his later output. Recent research on Schindler, the most exhaustive to date, places the house firmly in context, not as an anomaly but as a progenitor of a principled career. Its riches are undeniable and, today, revered by the initiated. Since its comparatively recent "discovery," it has been published internationally and a legion of architects, among whom Frank Gehry is the dominant figure, continues to pay homage. Even Philip Johnson made amends.[6]

Robert Sweeney
Judith Sheine

THE KINGS ROAD HOUSE

ROBERT SWEENEY

SCHINDLER'S VIENNA

R. M. SCHINDLER was among the least autobiographical of modern architects. He was born in Vienna in an age of reform that developed partly out of the nineteenth-century Industrial Revolution. His trail in Vienna led to the progressive architects Otto Wagner and Adolf Loos, and in America to Frank Lloyd Wright; yet what does one make of these platinum-coated associations? While it is possible to reconstruct the early years in some detail—Schindler's Vienna is remarkably intact physically, and his school records have largely survived—many questions, especially concerning the association with Loos, remain unanswered. Even his name provokes inquiry.

Schindler wasn't Schindler. He was christened Rudolf Michael Schlesinger in Vienna's sixth-district parish church, St. Ägyd Gumpendorf, two weeks after his birth on September 10, 1887. His father, Rudolf Israel Schlesinger (1859–1940), was of Jewish descent; his mother, Franziska Hertl (1863–1952), was Catholic. One week before their marriage in February 1887, Schlesinger converted to Catholicism.

Schlesinger is an opaque figure. He was born in Prague and at some point migrated to Vienna; he is identified in early documents as a *Reisender* (traveler) and *Geschaeftsreisender* (traveling salesman) and later as a *Kaufmann* (merchant). He spent ten months in America in 1880 and 1881. Franziska Hertl was Viennese; for many years she had a millinery shop on Mariahilferstrasse, Vienna's great shopping street.

Between 1899 and 1906 Schlesinger *fils* attended the k.k. Staats-Realschule in sixth-district Vienna. His record was uneven; overall, he seldom rose above average. His best marks were in geometry and, by the time of graduation, freehand drawing. Potentially the most interesting aspect of this period is not his schoolwork but his name change: in 1901, the family name became Schindler. Several sources—a note appended to his birth record in

St. Ägyd; his 1902–3 school record; and a document completed by his father and filed with the registrar of the sixth district—confirm but do not explain the reason for the change.[1]

After graduation from the Staats-Realschule in 1906, Schindler entered the Bau-(Architektur)schule of the k.k. Technische Hochschule in Vienna. Carl König (1841–1915), a prolific designer in the late Viennese Baroque tradition, was the dominant personality there. König's biographer Markus Kristan credits him with the development of "a kind of Austrian national style"; the Philipp-Hof (1882–84) on Albertinaplatz is representative (fig. 1).[2] If Schindler was generally unaware of or unreceptive to König's work, he could not have ignored König's 1904 annex for the Technische Hochschule (fig. 2). In two decades, König's work had gravitated toward the prevailing Neoclassical style.

König's legacy is both as architect and as teacher. He taught at the Technische Hochschule for nearly half a century; Josef Frank (1885–1967) and Friedrich Kiesler (1890–1965) are among his most prominent students. Although König was the contemporary of Otto Wagner (1841–1918), his work was rooted in the past. In a 1901 speech he rejected the aesthetic reforms taking place in Vienna and advocated instead a continuation of the architecture of historicism.[3]

Schindler attended two of König's classes informally, one in 1908–9, the other in 1910–11. Although in July 1911 he was awarded the degree of Diplom-Ingenieur, Bauschule (architecture school), Schindler clearly felt the need to continue his education in a less conservative institution. In October 1910, before graduating from the Technische Hochschule, Schindler entered the k.k. Akademie der bildenden Künste (Academy of Fine Arts), atelier of Otto Wagner. Wagner had more political capital than any architect in Vienna; his reputation had secured him the appointment to the academy in 1894. Wagner was a bridge to Modernism, and Schindler clearly understood the significance of his work. Wagner began his practice in the late 1860s and participated in Vienna's great Ringstrasse development. His early work was primarily academic and, as Carl E. Schorske has commented, "gave little reason to suspect in Wagner a modernist in the making."[4] In 1899, he joined the Secession, a group of artists formed two years earlier who rejected the prevailing historicism. His later buildings—most notably the 1904–6 Post Office Savings Bank and his own second house of 1912–13—secured his lasting reputation.

In 1910, Wagner was about to retire: Schindler was a member of his last class. Schindler's final project, described in extant school records in very old-fashioned German, was a theoretical "dead field" (cemetery) "in a great manner" for a city of five million people: it was a combination of Wagnerian rationalism and Beaux Arts fantasy. The document notes that he solved the task with talent and great diligence. He received a certificate of completion on July 1, 1913.[5]

During the same period, 1910–13, Schindler came under the spell of the famously renegade architect Adolf Loos (1870–1933), attending lectures at Loos's informal architectural school *(Bauschule)*. Schindler later recalled "our wonderful evenings together." As much social commentator as architect, Loos was no grave keeper; his rejection of historical inheritance is often interpreted as the catalyst for the Schindler we celebrate today. Looking back in 1920, Schindler described Loos to Louis Sullivan:

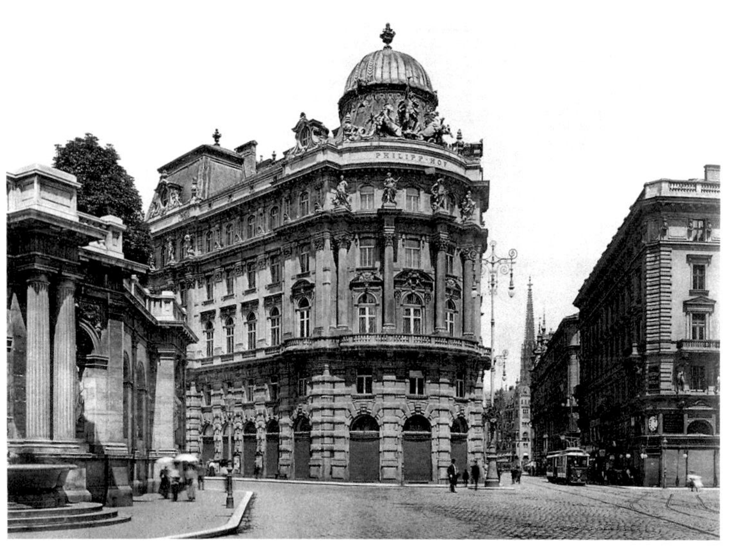

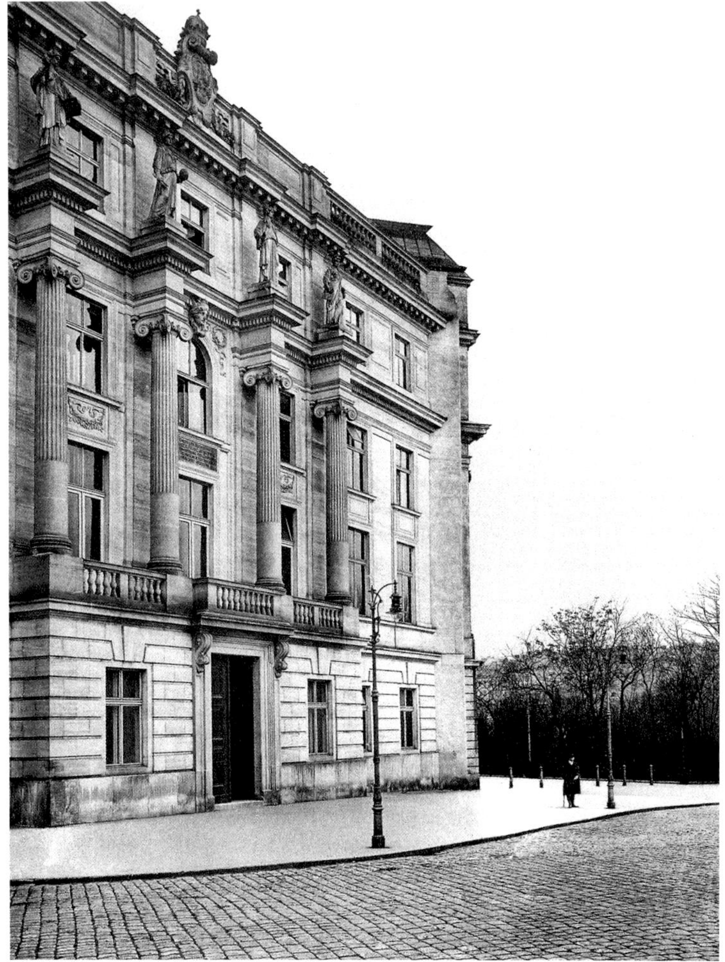

1 Carl König, Philipp-Hof, Vienna, 1882–84. From Markus Kristan, *Carl König 1841–1915* (Vienna: Verlag Holzhausen, 1999), p. 58.

2 Carl König, Technische Hochschule Annex, Vienna, 1904. From Markus Kristan, *Carl König 1841–1915* (Vienna: Verlag Holzhausen, 1999), p. 103.

> I must tell you all I happen to know about Mr. Loos. His is *[sic]* born in Austria [*sic:* Moravia] but one of the greatest influences on his life seem to be the few years of his youth he spent in America. The result of this trip was a series of articles he published in a Vienna paper, giving an analysis of the modern aims and characteristics of the manners, architecture and life of the Western World.
>
> He spent many years in Vienna as Architect, doing mostly interior decorating and forming the only serious opponent against the architectural atrocities of the "Secession."
>
> At that time I visited the school of Otto Wagner and took up the fight for Loos inside of this group. Wagner was about to resign his position on account of his age, and I proposed to him to recommend Loos as his successor. A few of us got in touch with Loos, and as it seemed impossible for him to get the nomination, he resolved to start his own school.[6]

Between September 1911 and February 1914, while still a student, Schindler worked for the architectural firm of Hans Mayr and Theodor Mayer in Vienna. Mayr (1877–1919) had attended the Wagnerschule from 1899 to 1902; his student projects, *Entwurf für eine Aussichtswarte auf dem Satzberge* (building for a viewpoint) and *Entwurf für ein Hotel* (hotel façade), were published in 1900.[7] He went on to become one of the most visible of Wagner's students; his work appeared frequently in *Der Architekt* and other journals. He first worked in an accomplished Jugendstil (Art Nouveau) manner that evolved into a version of academic classicism. His executed work included houses, restaurants, and a significant church in Bielitz (now Bielsko), Poland.

By 1910 Mayr had formed a partnership with Theodor Mayer, about whom no biographical information has come to light. Possibly Mayr felt he was losing touch with the work of the younger generation: while working with Mayer and Schindler, Mayr's work moved decisively toward Modernism. Two works of 1912, the Handelsschule Allina (Allina commercial school) and the Haus des österreichischen Bühnenvereines (actor's clubhouse), both in Vienna, reflect the transition. The five-story school employs a version of the base-column-capital composition typical of early skyscraper design; ornamentation is kept to a minimum (fig. 3). Though less resolved than contemporary work in Wagner's studio (to which the great corner panel clearly pays homage), the school is a clear indication of new directions for Mayr and Mayer. The actor's clubhouse is another five-story composition with a penthouse (fig. 4). Its ground floor, with its rhythm of posts and octagonal bay windows and, especially, the cantilevered entrance canopy—which appears to anticipate Mies van der Rohe—is remarkably modern. The upper stories are less architectonic, suggesting a building in transition. This is the earliest executed building with which Schindler can be associated. His role is clarified in a letter from Hans Mayr which explains that in addition to other work, he worked on construction supervision of the Actor's Club.[8]

Schindler's break came in early 1914. General consensus is that he had seen the magisterial portfolios *Ausgeführte Bauten und Entwürfe von Frank Lloyd Wright,* published in Berlin by Wasmuth in 1911, and wanted to work for Wright. The argument is plausible: a set purchased by the Technische Hochschule that year remains there today. He secured employment with a Chicago firm, Ottenheimer, Stern and Reichert, through an

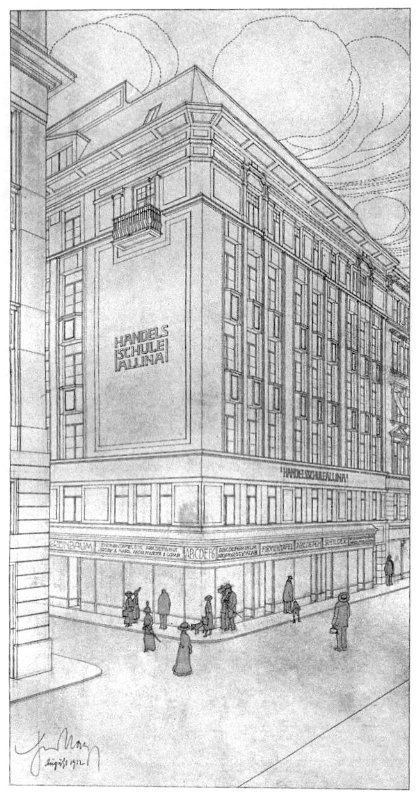

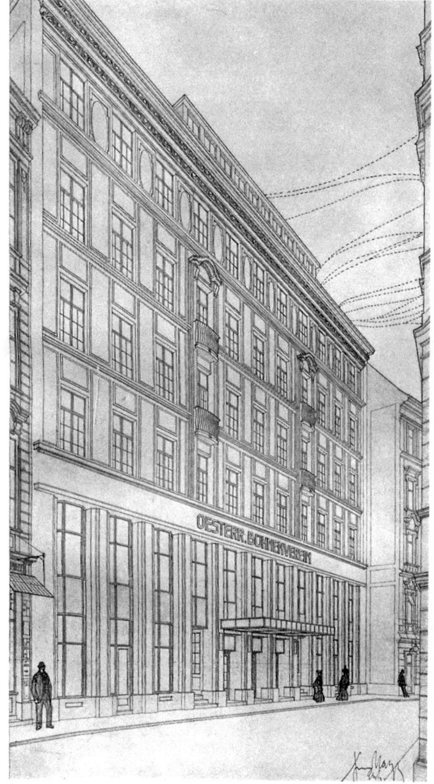

3 *(left)* Hans Mayr, Handelsschule Allina, Vienna, 1912. *Der Architekt* 19 (1913): pl. 62.

4 *(right)* Hans Mayr, Haus des österreichischen Bühnenvereines, Vienna, 1912. *Der Architekt* 19 (1913): pl. 64.

advertisement in a local newspaper.[9] Schindler resigned from Mayr and Mayer on February 10 and sailed from Hamburg on February 26 aboard the *Kaiserin Auguste Victoria,* four months before the assassination of Archduke Franz Ferdinand at Sarajevo, which led directly to the outbreak of World War I.

AMERICA

Schindler arrived at Ellis Island on March 7; in a letter to his friend and former classmate Richard Neutra (1892–1970), he described the experience as a "trip into a strange new life."[10] Within two weeks he was in Chicago. The work with Ottenheimer, Stern and Reichert proceeded as planned, but Schindler's sights were elsewhere. In late November he wrote to Frank Lloyd Wright:

> During the summer I tried several times without success to meet you. . . . I am a young architect, a pupil of Otto Wagner in Vienna and startet 8 months ago for this country with the intention to study the development of the American architectur. I succeeded in getting a position, but I can't help to feel very unhappy in an average American office. This feeling is growing from day to day and my only hope is to come in touch with you. So I ask if you could admit me to your office or give an opportunity to study your finished works at a close range.[11]

Wright responded two weeks later, inviting Schindler to his office. He also arranged for Schindler to visit Mrs. Avery Coonley's house in Riverside, Illinois, "the best I could then do in the way of a house." Wright finally agreed to hire Schindler in October 1917, indicating to his staff that Schindler would be in charge of his office during his absence.[12]

Wright's chief projects at the time were the Imperial Hotel in Tokyo and the ongoing development of Olive Hill in Hollywood for Aline Barnsdall. Correspondence between Wright and Schindler makes clear their evolving relationship. Initially Schindler was asked to supply information about building materials and equipment. Over time he became involved in the design process of the hotel, various buildings for Miss Barnsdall and other, smaller projects, and increasingly he fell victim to Wright's vitriol. In one letter, he was admonished by Wright: "Regarding the prospective clients—'Schindler' is keeping my *office* and my *work* for me in my absence. He has no identity as 'Schindler' with clients who want '*Wright*' . . . the natural thing would be . . . to lay it out as nearly as you can as I would do it and send it here for straightening."[13]

Wright's Chicago office was in the Monroe Building, designed by Holabird & Roche and completed in 1912, but his physical and emotional center of gravity was Taliesin in Spring Green, Wisconsin. Schindler made several extended visits to Taliesin and was photographed there (fig. 5) in 1918 by Julius Floto (1866–1951), an engineer who was working with Wright on the Imperial Hotel in Tokyo. Schindler left no written impressions of these visits, but Wright was a well-known collector of Asian art and, analyzing the Kings Road house, one can easily assume that Schindler assimilated some of the spirit.

In the spring of 1919, Schindler met Sophie Pauline Gibling, who within three months became his wife. Schindler's marriage was as progressive as his architectural affiliations. Pauline came out of Smith College, class of 1915, with an abiding, lifelong interest in social activism. She spent the summers of 1914 and 1915 working in the Boston slums; in September 1915 she became a "summer resident" at Jane Addams's Hull-House in Chicago. Pauline's activist instincts were equaled by a passion for music; late in life, she recalled first meeting Schindler at a performance of Prokofiev's barbaric *Scythian Suite,* which had premiered three years earlier in St. Petersburg. Greatly aroused, they "couldn't stay for the von Weber."[14]

The Schindlers' marriage on August 29 coincided with rabid political ferment in Chicago. A National Emergency Convention of the Socialist Party, fraught with dispute and "a flood of oratory," quickly fragmented and from the chaos the Communist Labor Party of America was organized. Its stated aim was "the overthrow of the present system of production in which the working class is mercilessly exploited, and the creation of an

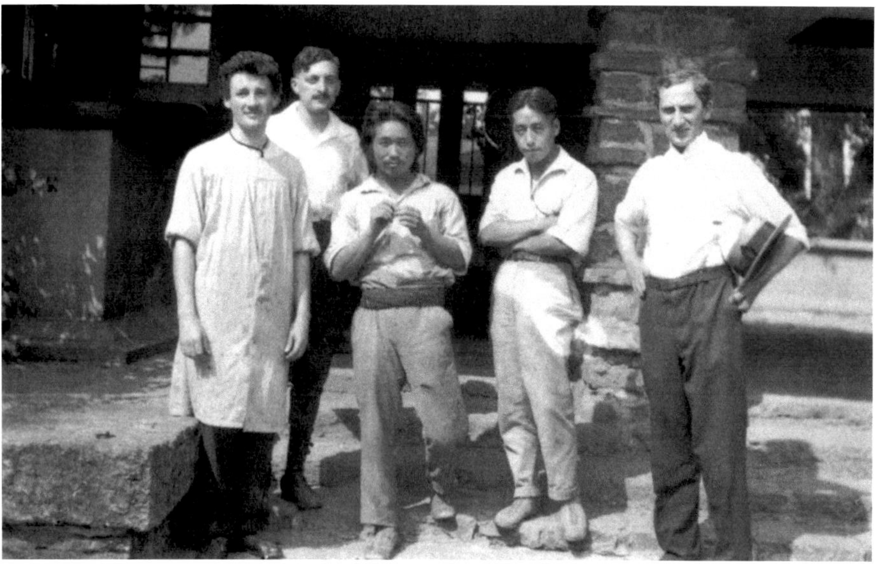

5 Julius Floto, photograph of R. M. Schindler (second from left), Taliesin, Spring Green, Wisconsin, 1918. Courtesy of Catherine Floto Loverud.

industrial republic." Analyzing the events, the *New York Times* concluded, "the new Communist Party in Chicago, [is] composed, it seems, largely of those so-called Socialists to whom admission to the Socialist Convention was denied." Although Pauline's fervor was probably far stronger than Schindler's, she spoke for both of them in declaring a short time later to her parents, "We are Communists!"[15]

The Schindlers lived for a time in Wright's own house in Oak Park and also traveled together to Taliesin; the experience had a profound effect on Pauline:

> I am with my comrade at the home of Mr. Frank Lloyd Wright. . . . Taliesin is a great estate,—a farm, an architectural studio, and a wonderfully beautiful home,—all in one. . . . The interiors, especially of Mr. Wright's private apartments, are like nothing I have ever seen. One walks into the rooms with a hush,—so highly-distilled is their beauty. . . . I can easily believe that Taliesin holds the highest beauty in America. . . .
>
> We . . . lead a really simple and primitive life in spite of all its beauty. For do not think, Ruth Imogene, that R.M.S. and I would accept lives of luxury. We are serious communists,—what people call Bolsheviki.

Schindler must have discussed his political activity with Frank Lloyd Wright, prompting Wright to respond, "Your pragmatic mind is good soil for Bolshevism."[16]

Threaded throughout the dialogue between Wright and Schindler was the prospect of work in Los Angeles, both the completion of the Barnsdall development and new projects. In a letter sent from Tokyo on February 9, 1920, Wright indicated to Schindler, "I still look toward Los Angeles as a place in which I might turn your services to good account but I know nothing—*absolutely nothing* of what is going on there."[17] Undeterred, Schindler wired Wright on April 17, "Going west May," and Wright responded nine days later, "Not needed west before my return."[18] The sparring continued until late November, when the Schindlers finally left for California.

"BOLD AND NOVEL CONSTRUCTION"[19]

The Schindlers arrived in Los Angeles on December 3, 1920, and began almost at once looking for a place to build a house. At first they wanted to live in Pasadena, "for we don't like Hollywood, except in the little canyons between steep mountain or hill ranges." By mid December they were intending to "build on a slope looking toward [mountains] . . . perhaps by spring'; in January they had found "perfect spots for our studio."[20] No immediate decision was made, however.

The concept of a communal lifestyle must have jelled shortly after Marian Da Camara—Pauline's classmate at Smith College—and her husband, Clyde Chace, arrived in Los Angeles in July 1921. Pauline and Marian had worked together in Boston and Chicago and continued their correspondence after their marriages. Marian expressed a strong lay interest in architecture, and both she and Clyde were "taken into" the work of Irving Gill; the opportunity to work with him prompted the move west. By November the two couples—Schindler and Chace—had decided to build together.[21] They purchased property on Kings Road, a 100 × 200 foot site in the then-unincorporated flatlands between Hollywood and Beverly Hills. Schindler justified the decision in economic terms:

> In order to further my professional ends I have to go into a middleclass section . . . the owners who have their residences across from us (one block of ground each) want to built up their surroundings nicely—and are not specially after the money—but after desirable neighbors. By dividing the lot with the Chases *[sic]* each of us takes the responsibility for only \$1375^{00} for which we could not get anything desirable anywheres.[22]

Schindler designed the house over a two-month period, in November and December 1921; Pauline noted that the details were "worked out . . . in our many ardent conferences together." The house was to be "one architectural unit"; one wing for the Schindlers, another for the Chaces, "with certain utilities in common, and . . . also a third studio, to be rented out."[23]

There were four distinct phases in the planning process, each a logical development of a theme. Schindler began with a pinwheel configuration that provided different orientations for each unit of the house: apartments for each family and a guest, a strategy consistent throughout the design development and one that he repeated in 1923 at Pueblo Ribera Court, twelve vacation cottages in La Jolla, California. In the first version (fig. 6), the wings for the Schindlers and the Chaces—called "studios" in his plans—were accessible only

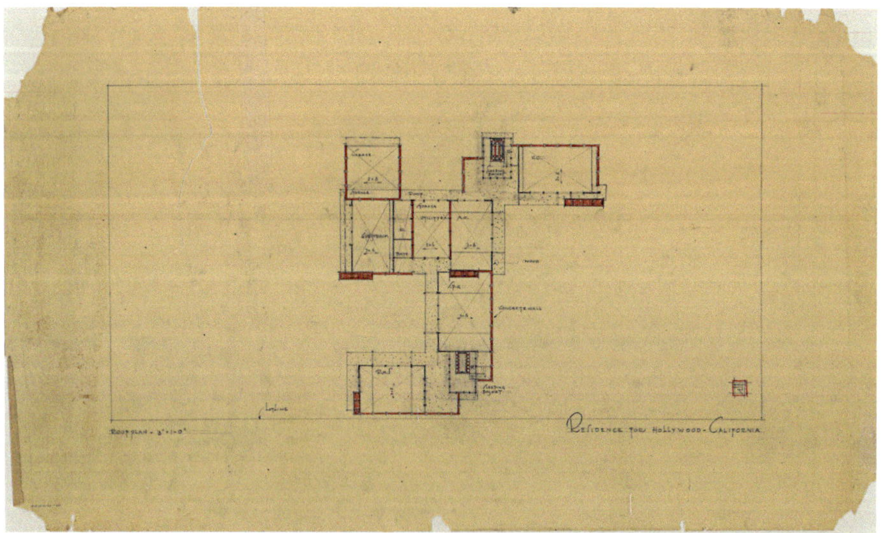

6 Schindler, Residence for Hollywood, California, scheme 1. Rudolph M. Schindler Collection, Architecture and Design Collection, Art, Design & Architectural Museum, University of California, Santa Barbara.

from outside corridors. The second scheme, dated November 1921, very nearly approximates the house as it was built except that Schindler has indicated the layout for one family with conventional designations for the studios: living room, dining room, and two bedrooms (fig. 7). Another plan shows how the "building may be converted into a room residence by adding a few partitions" (fig. 8).

The final scheme, shown in a pair of singularly unlovely drawings, is dated December 1921 (figs. 9 and 10). In this plan, a nursery defined by low walls has been incorporated into Clyde's studio in anticipation of the arrival of the Chaces' first child. Expecting to begin construction at once, and again emphasizing economy, Schindler explained that the house would be built "as small and as cheaply as possible—$7000—for two families makes $3500^{00} for each—an amount for which it would be impossible to build separately."[24]

A decade later he described the program thus:

> A cooperative dwelling for two young couples. . . .
>
> The ordinary residential arrangement providing rooms for specialized purposes has been abandoned.
>
> Instead, each person receives a large private studio; each couple, a common entrance hall and bath. Open porches on the roof are used for sleeping. An enclosed patio for each couple, with an out-of-door fire place, serves the purposes of an ordinary living room. The form of the house divides the garden into several such private rooms. A separate guest apartment, with its own garden, is also provided for. One kitchen is planned for both couples.[25]

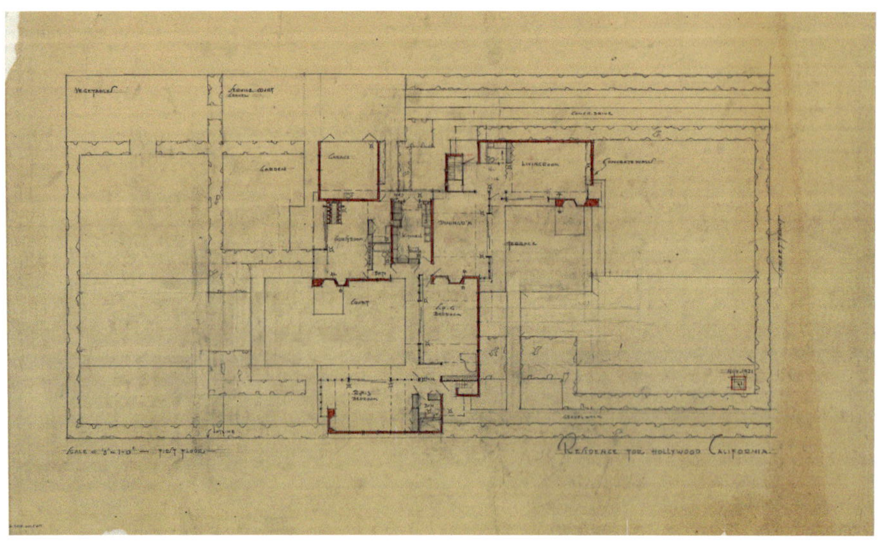

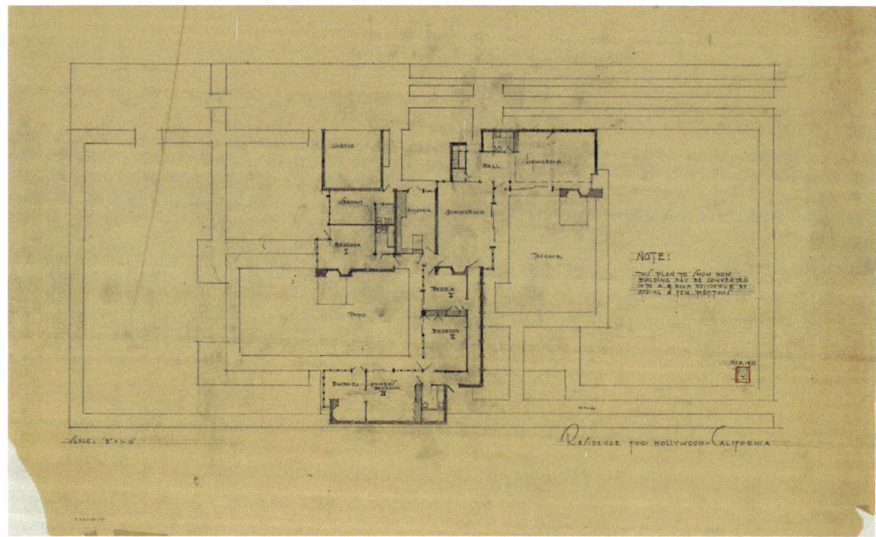

7 *(above top)* Schindler, Residence for Hollywood, California, scheme 2, November 1921. Rudolph M. Schindler Collection, Architecture and Design Collection, Art, Design & Architecture Museum, University of California, Santa Barbara.

8 *(above bottom)* Schindler, Residence for Hollywood, California, scheme 3, November 1921. Rudolph M. Schindler Collection, Architecture and Design Collection, Art, Design & Architecture Museum, University of California, Santa Barbara.

9 *(opposite above)* Schindler, Residence for C. C. & R. M. S. to be erected in Hollywood—Cal—Floor Plan, scheme 4, December 1921. Rudolph M. Schindler Collection, Architecture and Design Collection, Art, Design & Architecture Museum, University of California, Santa Barbara.

10 *(opposite below)* Schindler, Residence for C. C. & R. M. S. to be erected in Hollywood—Cal—Elevations, December 1921. Rudolph M. Schindler Collection, Architecture and Design Collection, Art, Design & Architecture Museum, University of California, Santa Barbara.

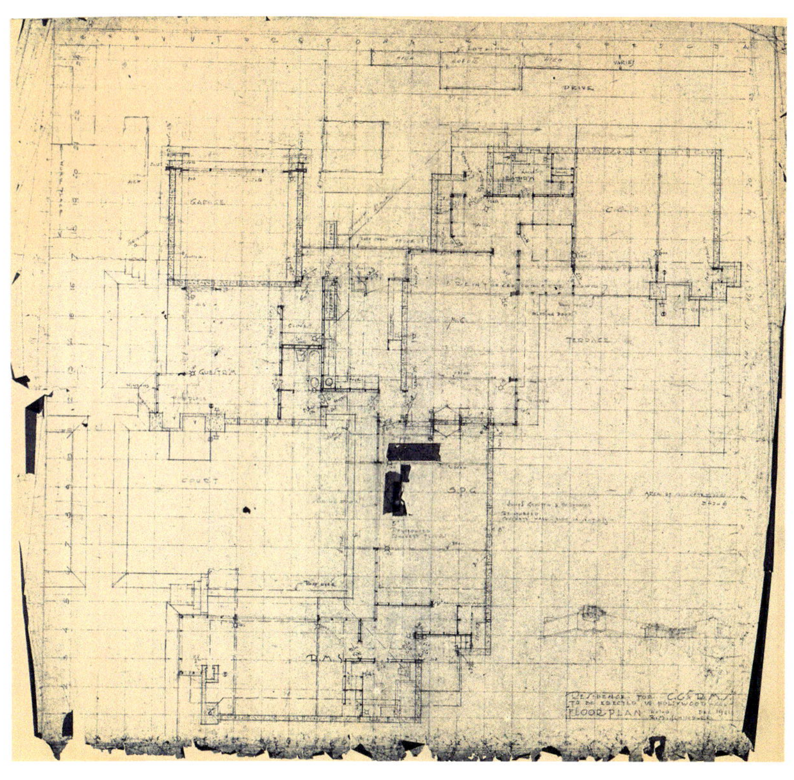
DRIVE
GARAGE
COURT
TERRACE
FLOOR PLAN

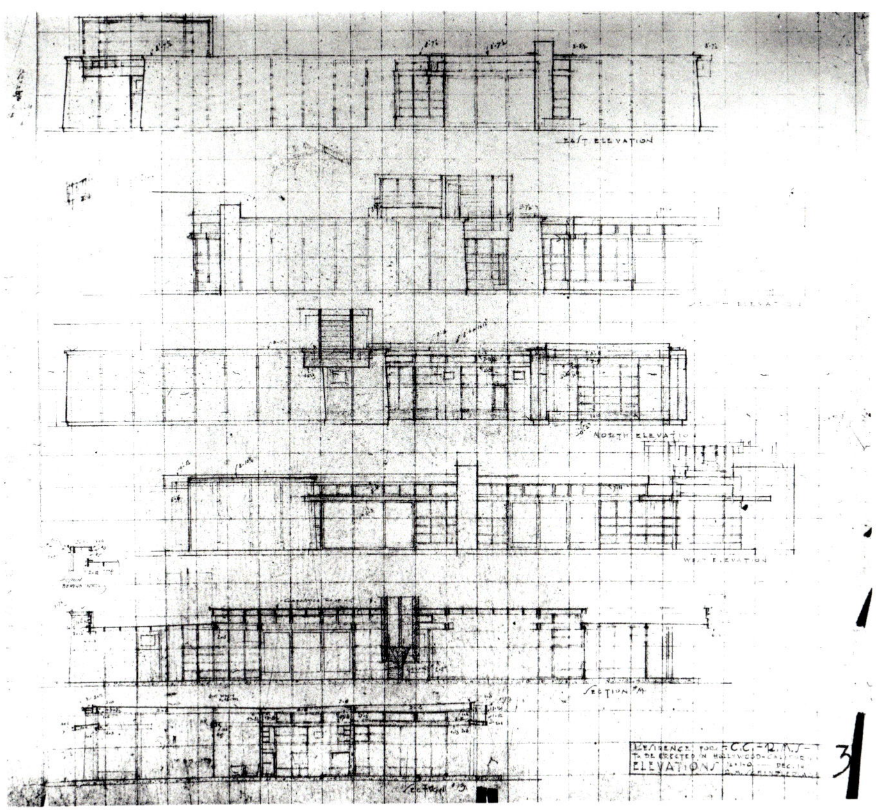
EAST ELEVATION
NORTH ELEVATION
WEST ELEVATION
ELEVATIONS

The house was constructed using Schindler's Slab-Tilt system—readily legible in the plans and elevations—in which reinforced concrete wall units, cast on the concrete slab floor, were hoisted into position using a tripod, block, and tackle. Schindler did not invent this system, and analogy with the work of Irving Gill is inevitable. Whether Gill was the catalyst is impossible to say, though he had used a similar system in his 1914 La Jolla Woman's Club, and he and Schindler had met by April 1921. Nonetheless, there are significant technical modifications and formal advances at Kings Road. Gill cast entire walls as units, which were lifted with machinery. Schindler divided the walls into units four feet on center, which could theoretically be lifted by two men. He expressed the nature of the construction by filling the voids between the slabs—created by the formwork—with glass, animating the walls and admitting light.

Although Schindler projected on January 4, "we shall begin to build next week," surviving documentation is rife with mentions of delays caused by rain. In the interim, he "made a perspective sketch of the studio,—all black and gold" (fig. 11). Describing it to her mother, Pauline observed, "Its severity of line makes it a monumental thing."[26]

Excavation finally began in late February; Pauline described the experience:

> We've had the jolliest afternoon, digging trenches! Yes . . . . The lot at King's *[sic]* Road seems to lie in the middle of all space. First we look up to the Hollywood Range, which lies from Pasadena to the sea; and then in the lower direction, we look over miles of quiet space..And now and then, as you dig your trench, and throw the spadefuls of good brown earth up, you here a meadow-lark singing. And you stop just at sunset, which is again a wide, lovely thing, and warms you with the thought of how the sunsets are to be watched from the windows of R.M.S's studio.[27]

Two weeks later, on March 7, Schindler reported significant progress and, like Pauline, alluded to both the romance and the hard work of building:

> Three days of coming home at 12 oclock—yesterday at 4 ocl. and now it is 2 in the morning—having spent both nights finishing concrete floors with Clyde—with stars and lights all around us—except our two rooms all floors are down now—and I sat carefully today smoothing your threshold towards the kitchen.

Schindler followed up four days later:

> I worked on the house all day—helping out as a "laborer" at the concrete mixer—all walls and floors are cast, exsepting the ones of our two studios—a sign is up announcing the "Slab-Tilt" construction.[28]

Optimism aside, the project continued to be plagued by rain: "the other day—after working on our floorfinish until 2 oclock in the morning, a sudden rain spoiled quite a portion of it." And the next day it was "raining again—and poor Chase *[sic]* is probably stomping around

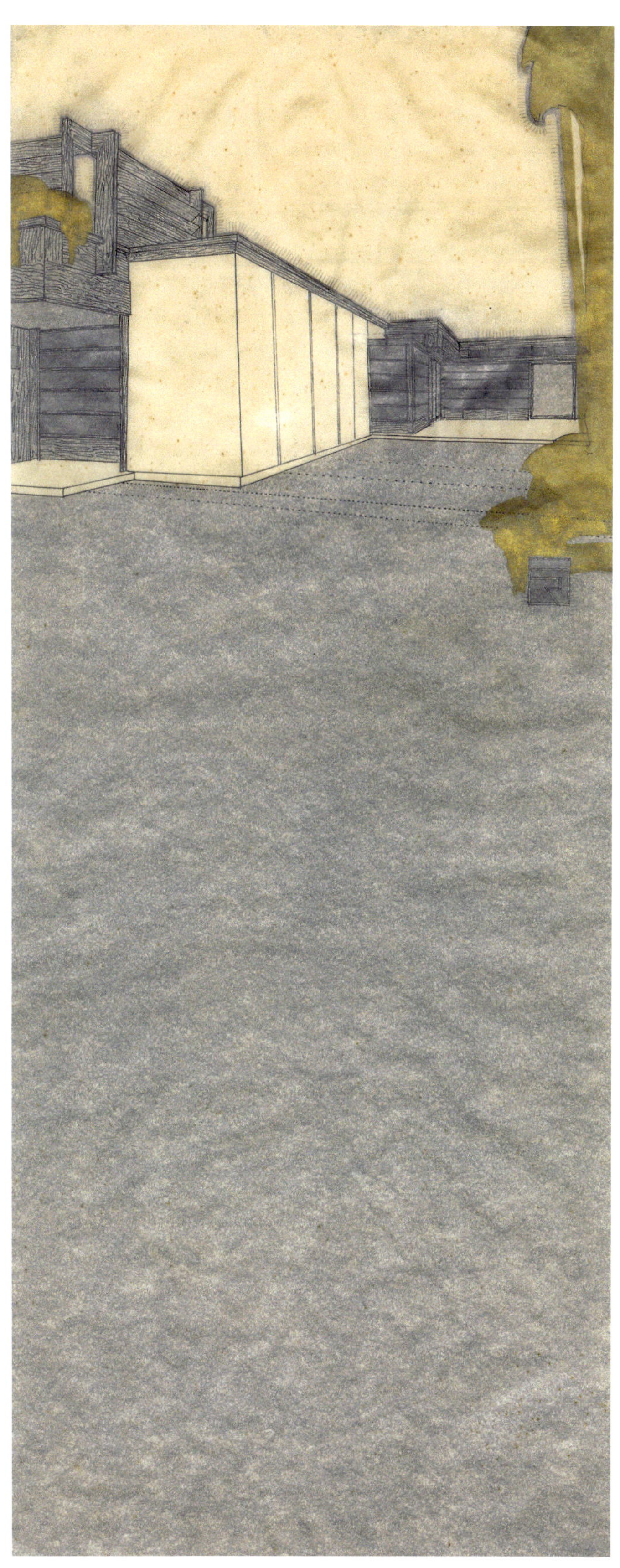

11 Schindler, watercolor perspective of the Kings Road house, ca. February 1922. Rudolph M. Schindler Collection, Art, Design & Architecture Museum, University of California, Santa Barbara.

in the mud. He is very faithful to the job and has done very well in spite of the weather—I remember last year we lost only one week thru rain—this year it is already four. However it was not possible to wait—and another two weeks will see the walls being tilted up—which will end the concrete work." Nonetheless, already Schindler was "quite satisfied, the house will be a success—inspite of the many innovations involved."[29]

The garage and guest studio walls were up by April 4, and carpentry work began soon after (figs. 12, 13, 14). Structurally the house is a combination of the concrete wall slabs and a simple post-and-beam system. The roof construction consists of 3 × 8 inch redwood beams, two feet on center, exposed on the interior and covered with redwood shiplap (fig. 15, below left). It is supported on one side of each studio by a concrete wall, on the other by two wooden posts. Pairs of beams, 6 feet 2 inches above the floor and spanning each room, extend to the exterior to support cantilevered overhangs. The beams also support sliding pendant lights with paper shades; otherwise, they are nonstructural. Partitions and windows are nonsupporting redwood frames constructed of thin studs, extending from floor to ceiling, and rails—Schindler called them muntin bars—filled with glass or Universal Insulite, an insulation board made of pressed sugarcane, and held in place with "stops" (battens) (fig. 15, below right). Sliding screens in each studio opening to patios were canvas stretched in mahogany frames.

The deceptive simplicity—borne out in recent restoration work—of Schindler's scheme became clear early in the building process. On April 14 he wrote, "Guestroom being covered . . . but Clyde is slow—it will take five weeks yet I presume." He followed up a week later: "Clyde can not get carpenters—two came today—looked the job over—got scared—and ran—." They also ran afoul of the technology of the building system: on April 22 Schindler told Pauline, "now a few slabs won't 'tilt'—they stick—and we shall have to use wedges—otherwise the good news that another carpenter is making a try—garage, kitchen & guestroom roofed over—plumber starting Monday."[30]

One significant change, a reconfiguration of the fireplaces in the S.P.G. and M.D.C. studios, was made to Schindler's plans during construction. As originally designed, the fireboxes were positioned side by side in the manner of those in the C.B.C. studio/Chace patio and the guest studio/Schindler patio (see figs. 7 and 8). The final back-to-back hexagonal design was indicated in the December 1921 drawings, but a subsequent note from Schindler to Pauline reveals that the sheet copper finally installed was a later decision. On March 20, he wrote, "Here is a question to be answered quickly—what color & texture brick for your fireplace . . . rough, smooth? yellow—tan—red—? Only colors of 'burned' clay are in place." Later, Schindler told Pauline that he was "trying to make a *copper* fireplace . . . no brick."[31]

As the house neared completion, Schindler fully addressed the garden. He had made oblique references in his early sketches: the garden clearly was to be an architectural extension of the house, though scant details were provided. Along the way, Marian Chace tried her hand; in March she was "very busy already with the garden,—both vegetable and landscape," though Schindler commented a short time later, "Kimi's garden not very successful—the soil is hard to handle."[32]

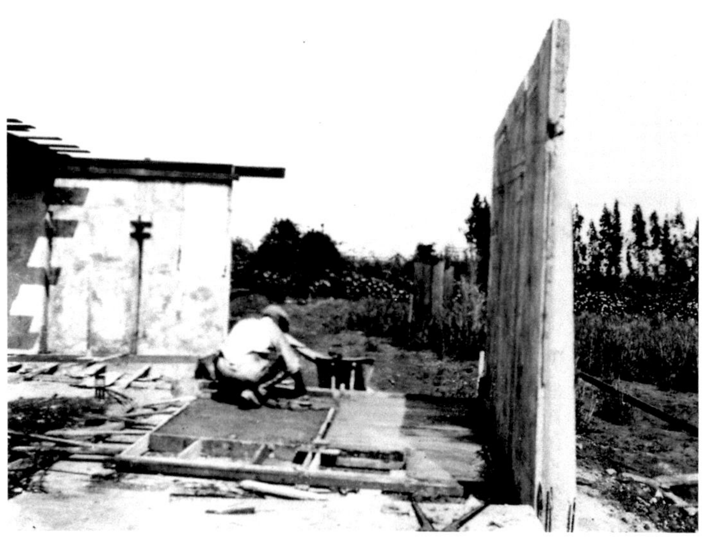

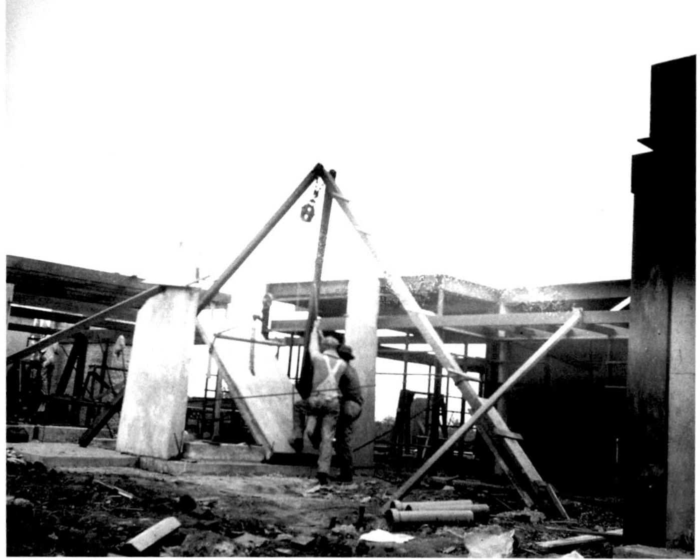

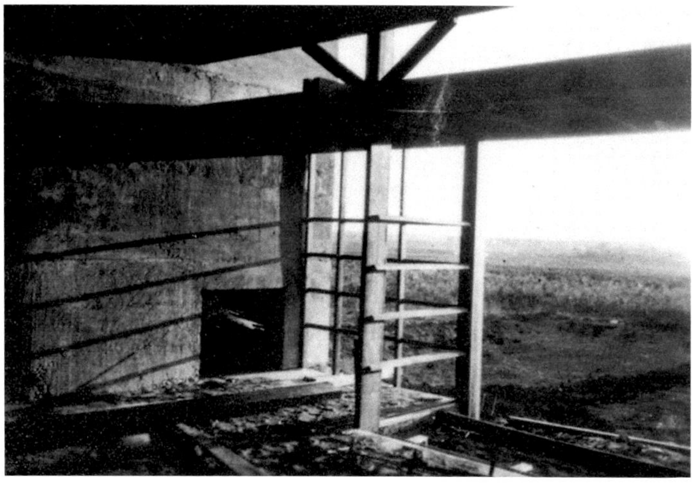

12 Concrete work, 1922. Photo courtesy of the Schindler Family Collection.

13 Slab-Tilt construction, 1922. Photo courtesy of the Schindler Family Collection.

14 Wood framing, 1922. Photo courtesy of the Schindler Family Collection.

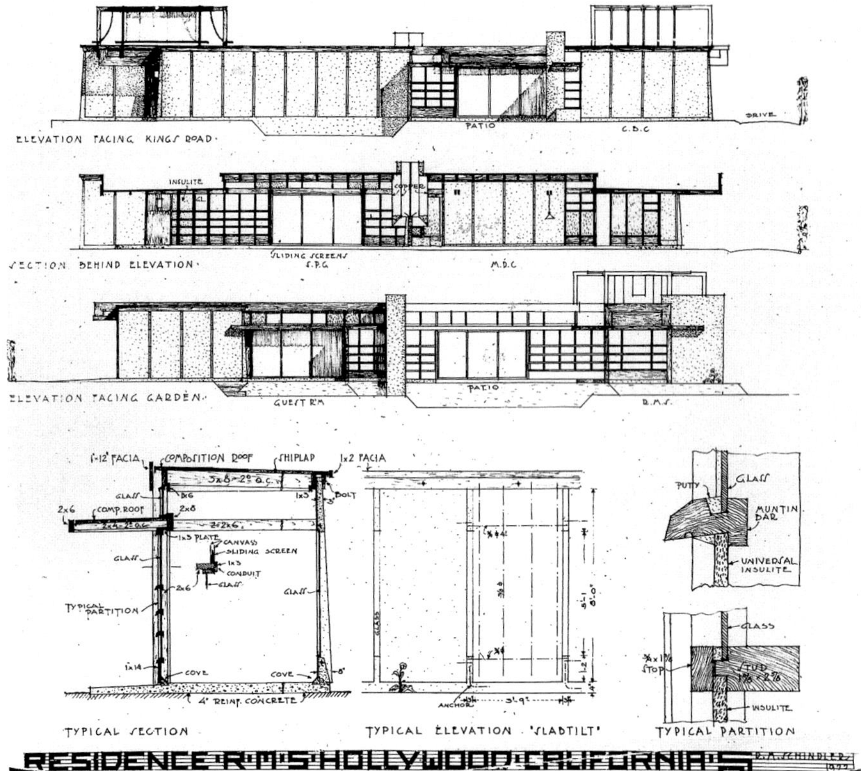

15 Schindler, Kings Road house elevations, sections, details. Rudolph M. Schindler Collection, Architecture and Design Collection, Art, Design & Architecture Museum, University of California, Santa Barbara.

The design had reached intellectual maturity by late April, when Pauline told her parents, "The latest blue-print . . . includes the plan of the landscaping, sunken gardens and all." This blueprint is lost, but another drawing, probably completed later, fully conveys the genius of the place. The entire half-acre site was conceived as self-contained living space, laid out in a series of sliding and interlocking planes (fig. 16). Nowhere in the history of landscape had there been a garden like this. Bamboo hedges along the eastern and southern property lines provide privacy from the street and neighbors. The garden is divided internally with clipped hedges and changes in ground level—sunken gardens—that control circulation and create outdoor rooms for each of the three apartments, Schindler, Chace, and guest. As Pauline's sister Dorothy observed later, the place was "a little nation all its own." She had "not been out of it for two days—yet we live so that it's really like living outdoors, so you hardly miss not going away."[33]

A completion permit for the Kings Road house was issued on June 6, 1922, though work continued for several weeks after the couples moved in. The garden as well was a slow

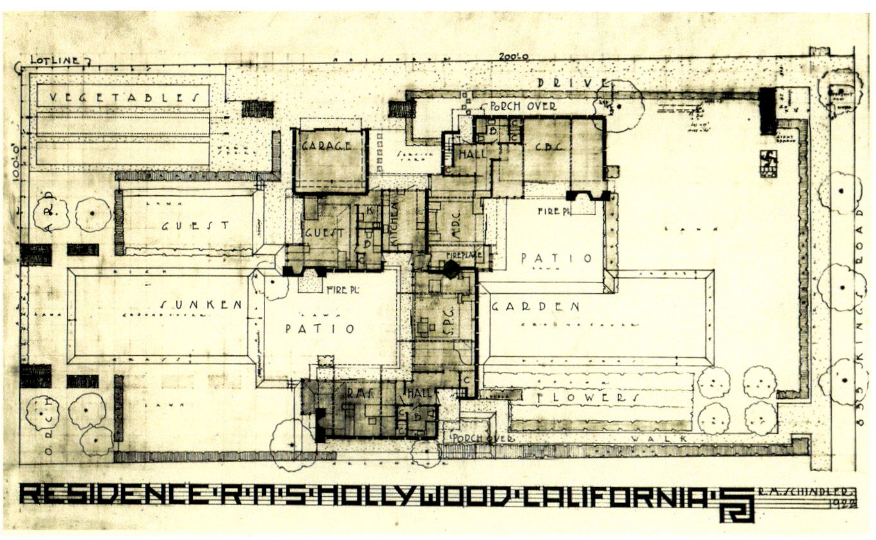

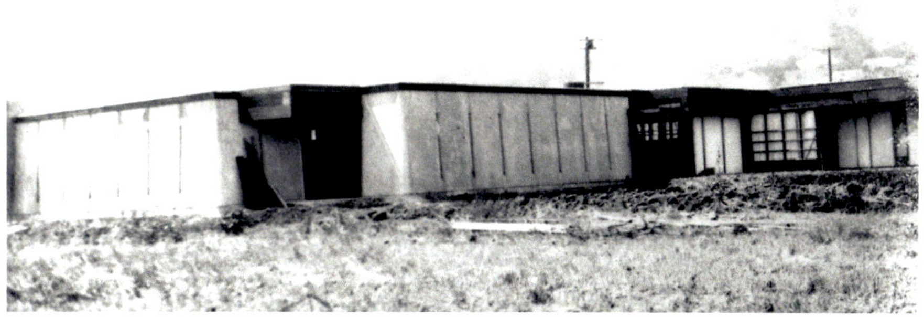

16 Schindler, Residence R. M. S. Hollywood, California, plan showing the gardens. Collection of Robert Sweeney.

17 Schindler, Kings Road house before April 1924. Photo courtesy of Anne Harriet Chace Eastwood.

process. Schindler indicated at the time that it was premature to publish photographs of the house "since none of the planting is done—which is absolutely necessary to complete the scheme" (fig. 17).[34] The guest studio was the first space in the house to be furnished; photographs taken in 1922 during Dorothy Gibling's occupancy give some indication of the aesthetics (figs. 18, 19). The finest early photographs of the house, taken in 1924 and lost to memory until recently, come from the archive of Swiss architect Werner Moser. The images provide extraordinary detail—the south (Schindler) sleeping porch, sometimes referred to by the Schindlers as a sleeping basket, has been enlarged to the west, the north basket is yet to be begun, and the original garage door is in place. Landscape work is under way—the stand of bamboo at the east end of the driveway and the Monterey cypress hedge are in place—but the garden overall is unkempt (figs. 20, 21, 22).

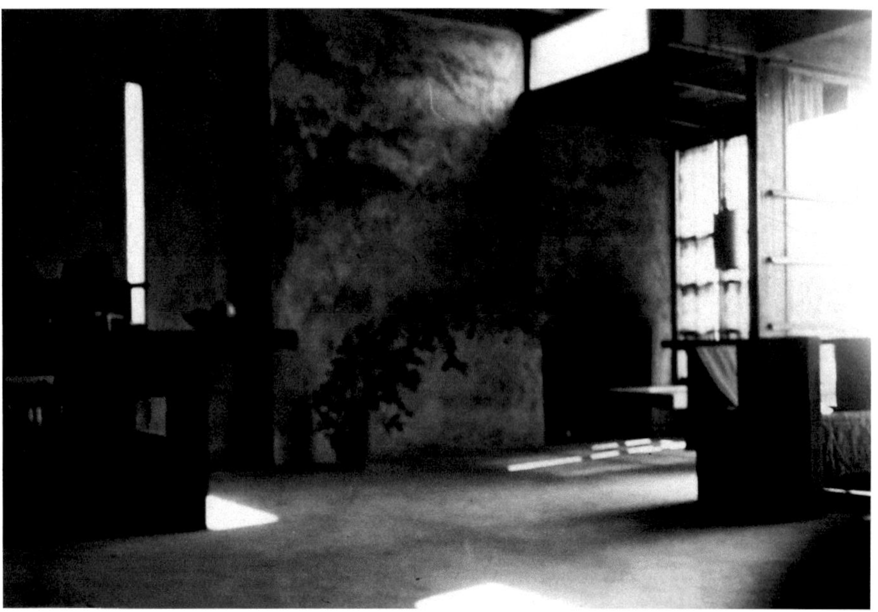

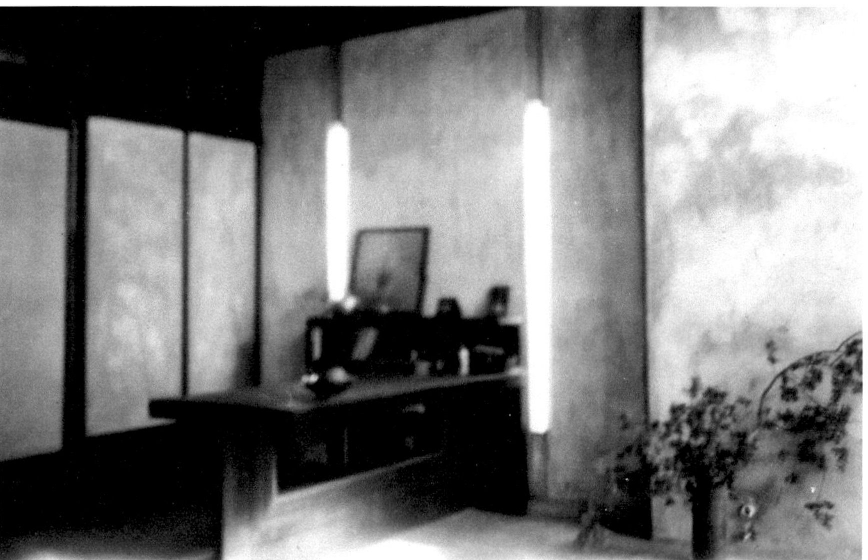

18 Kings Road house, guest studio looking southwest, August 1922. Photo included in correspondence from Dorothy S. Gibling to her parents; photographer unknown. Schindler Family Collection, courtesy of Friends of the Schindler House.

19 Kings Road house, guest studio looking southeast, August 1922. Photo included in correspondence from Dorothy S. Gibling to her parents; photographer unknown. Schindler Family Collection, courtesy of Friends of the Schindler House.

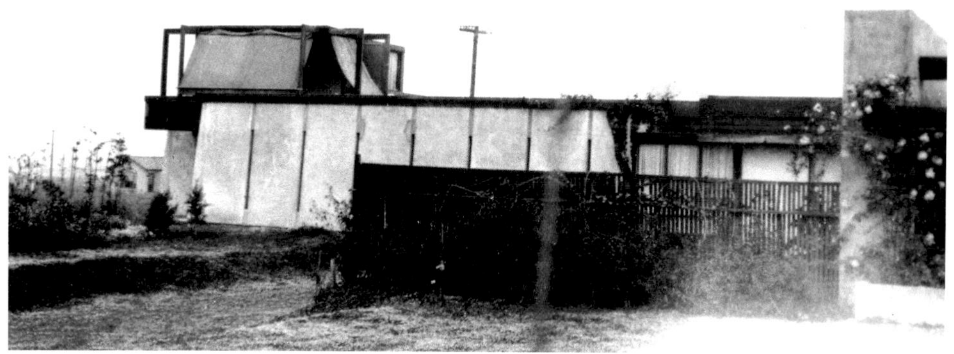

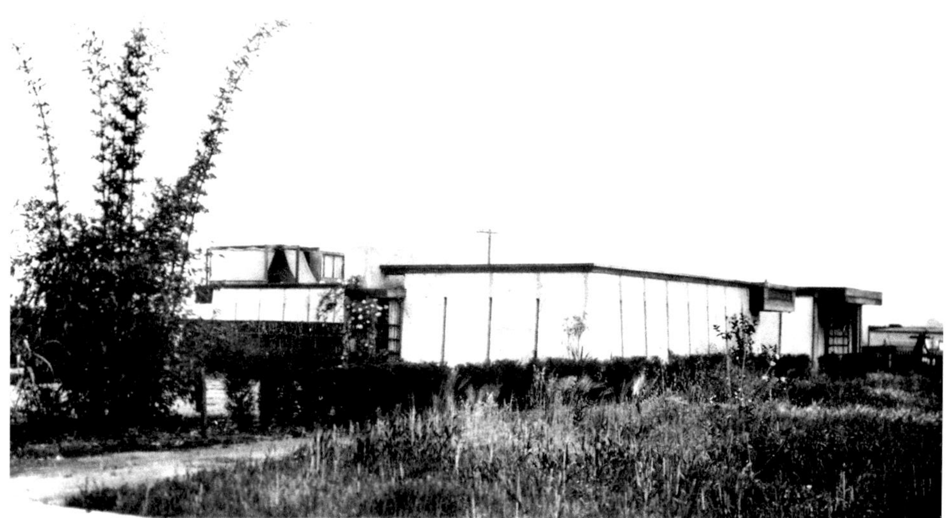

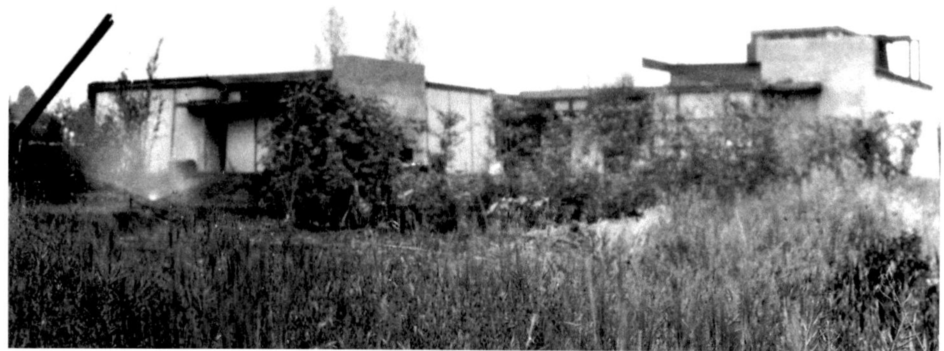

20 Kings Road house, east elevation, 1924. Archive Werner M. Moser, Eidgenossische Technische Hochschule Zürich.

21 Kings Road house from northeast, 1924. Archive Werner M. Moser, Eidgenossische Technische Hochschule Zürich.

22 Kings Road house from southwest, 1924. Archive Werner M. Moser, Eidgenossische Technische Hochschule Zürich.

About the same time, the house had a bit role—anonymous and upstaged—in a silent film. In four brief clips from *Sherlock, Jr.* (1924), Buster Keaton bicycles past, his comic gestures perhaps unwittingly providing an extraordinary glimpse of the house as it originally appeared in an open field with the Hollywood Hills in the background (fig. 23).

THE MOST IMPRACTICAL HOUSE IN THE WORLD

The Kings Road house is an extreme example of architectural ratiocination. Its bare-bones articulation is dictated by a spirit of reduction to an essence, not style per se. Schindler abandoned the traditional "onion-like . . . layers of finishing materials,—lath, plaster, paint, paper, hangings, etc.," and wove together "a few structural materials which retain their natural color and texture throughout." Concrete walls and floors were untreated; redwood ceilings and window and door frames were wire-brushed to accentuate the grain and coated with a mixture of unboiled linseed oil and turpentine. Schindler described the house as "the beginning of a building system which a highly developed technical science will permit in the future. Each material will take its place openly in the structure, fulfilling all architectural and structural requirements of its place in the organic fabric of the building."[35]

Although much is eliminated, there is no sense whatsoever of artistic impoverishment. Using a consistent four-foot module and one basic structural unit, the tilt-up wall slab, Schindler created forms and spaces of extraordinary variety and richness. No two rooms are alike; he described each as representing "a variation on one structural and architectural theme."[36] The house is particularly beautiful at night—a quality not lost on the Schindlers—with its soft lighting and seven fireplaces blazing.

What is missing is creature comfort. The philosophy that only what is beautiful is comfortable has limits. Like many experimental works of architecture, the house demands to be lived up to. Dorothy Gibling wanted none of it. In a moment of pique, she described the guest apartment—the most complete space in the house—to her parents in 1922: "I s'pose it's R.M.S.'s queer ideas that have gone to make my room so lovely—& so entirely in keeping—but to me they're most tremendously un understandable. When they interfere with comfort & peace of mind." Dorothy was at once more charitable and less convincing in describing conditions in mid August: "It still continues about a hundred and sixty five during the daytime—but . . . with six inch cement walls, the inside of this house stays reasonably cool."[37]

Coming from Vienna by way of Chicago, Schindler must have found the Southern California climate benign; still, there are extremes he did not take into account. The house can be insufferably hot—and very cold—and, as it was designed, there is no remediation. Numerous occupants have also left dismal reports of the leaking roof. The sleeping baskets, especially, seem optimistic. In 1924, Pauline described "a shattering wind that made sleeping for us upstairs seem like being up among the spanker-sails of a sailing-vessel."[38]

Attempts, especially by Pauline but also by Schindler himself, to correct physical shortcomings were unsuccessful. The house is finite; the rigor of the scheme precludes

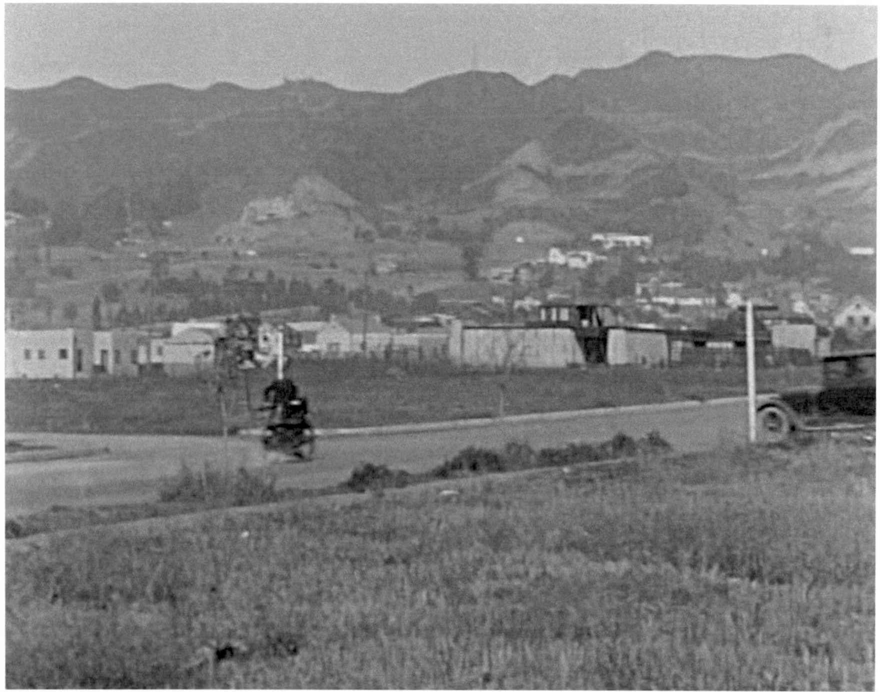

23 Buster Keaton, *Sherlock, Jr.*, 1924. Sherlock Jr. image courtesy The Rohauer Collection.

changes of any kind. The addition of the nursery to the Chace apartment—ostensibly under Schindler's supervision—seriously compromised the quality of light and space in the C.B.C. studio, the only one with two walls of concrete. The glazed bay, thematically consistent with the one in the R.M.S. studio, was blocked by the nursery walls; skylights were cut in as a makeshift. A nursery added to the west patio by Schindler in 1953 for his grandson, Eric, similarly intruded; it was removed in 1985. Pauline's changes over the years, including multiple layers of paint, wall paneling, floor coverings, enclosing the sleeping porches, and so on, made in the spirit of domesticity, suggest that the house was too radical even for her.

Today we honor the Schindlers' intellect, creative spirit, and lives at Kings Road. As an architectural laboratory, the house is unsurpassed. It is the birthplace of the Southern California Modernism so celebrated today. Schindler worked there until his death, pursuing new ideas based on an evolving ideology and creating a body of work as vital today as it was incomprehensible to the East Coast establishment ninety years ago. Richard Neutra—who lived at Kings Road with his wife, Dione, between 1925 and 1930 and who went on to surpass Schindler in quantity, if not inventiveness—had his finest moment here with his design for the iconic town house for Philip Lovell, the first brilliant expression of the International Style in America.

From the beginning, the house served as a salon. Dorothy Gibling described one evening:

> It's really too bad you couldn't have been here on Friday evening—for the recital—I never *dreamed* 835 could look so truly lovely *and* impressive. As folks rambled through the various rooms—& across the courts with their open fires—I'm sure quite several of them were highly impressed. At any rate, *I* was. There seemed to be hundreds of people—but probably not more than fifty or sixty—and such a mixture—from the most formal to the long haired variety, though Helen Barr & I were both rather disappointed to find how comparatively few really *funny* types there were! We knew no one so had planned to just watch the "passing show"—but were surprised rather by the high toned air of it all than the Bohemianism we had gleefully expected.[39]

Beginning in the early 1940s, activity at the house increasingly reflected Pauline Schindler's interest in radical social ferment. The *Index, Un-American Activities in California,* 1943–1961, reads like a roster of her friends and correspondents. John Howard Lawson (1894–1977), a blacklisted screenwriter, was the most prominent; shortly after his death he was identified as "the top Red in Hollywood." Others included Stephen H. Fritchman (1902–1981), under whose leadership the First Unitarian Church in Los Angeles became a center of liberal politics; Rose Chernin (1901–1995), executive secretary of the communist-backed American Committee for the Protection of the Foreign Born; and Berkeley Tobey (1881–1962), husband of Esther McCoy. Asked late in life about these associates, she responded, smiling, "They have all been here."[40]

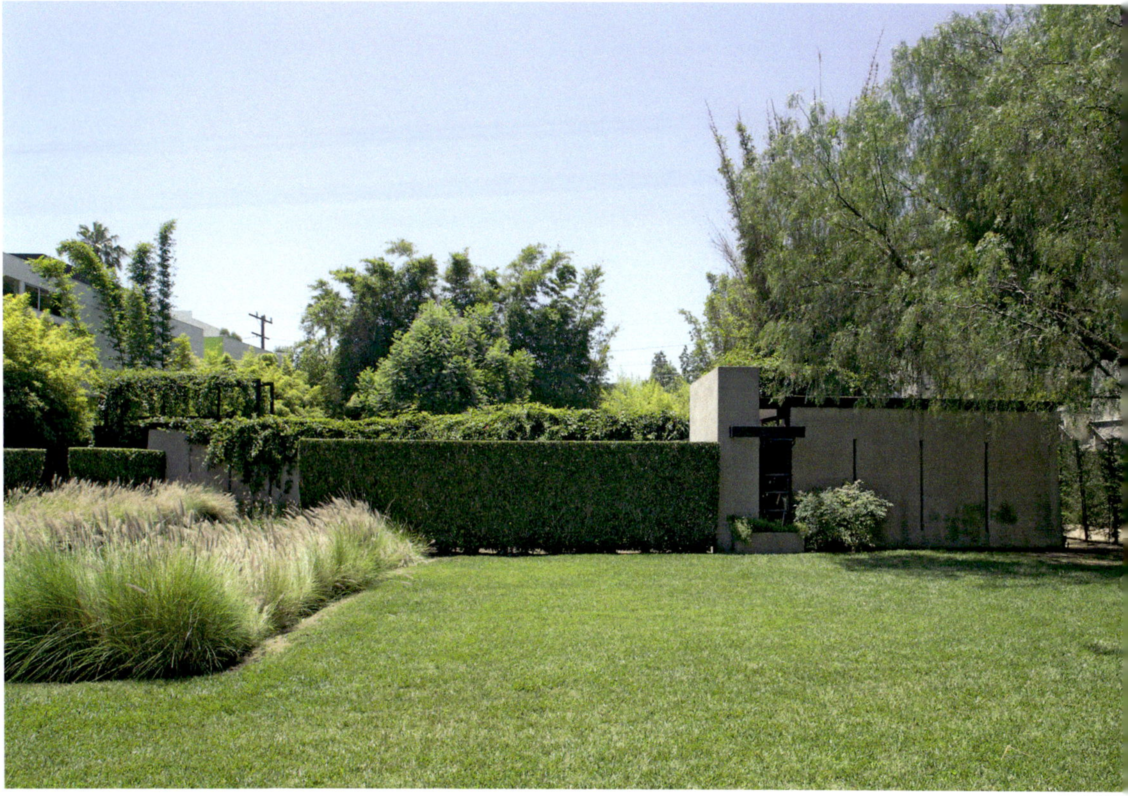

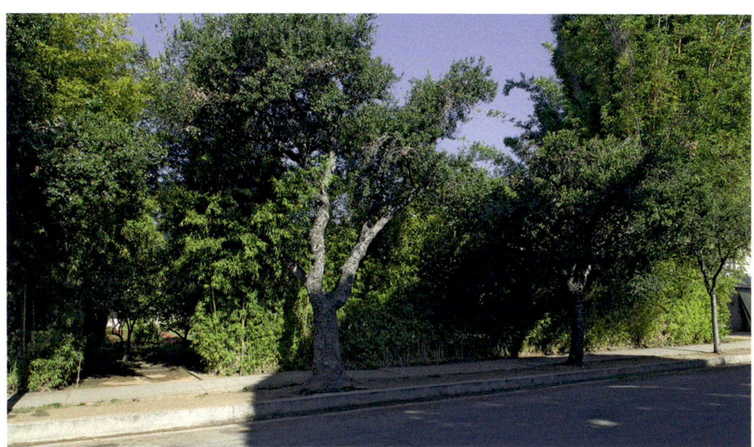

PLATE 1 Front garden, looking west.

PLATE 2 View from Kings Road of the Schindler House site.

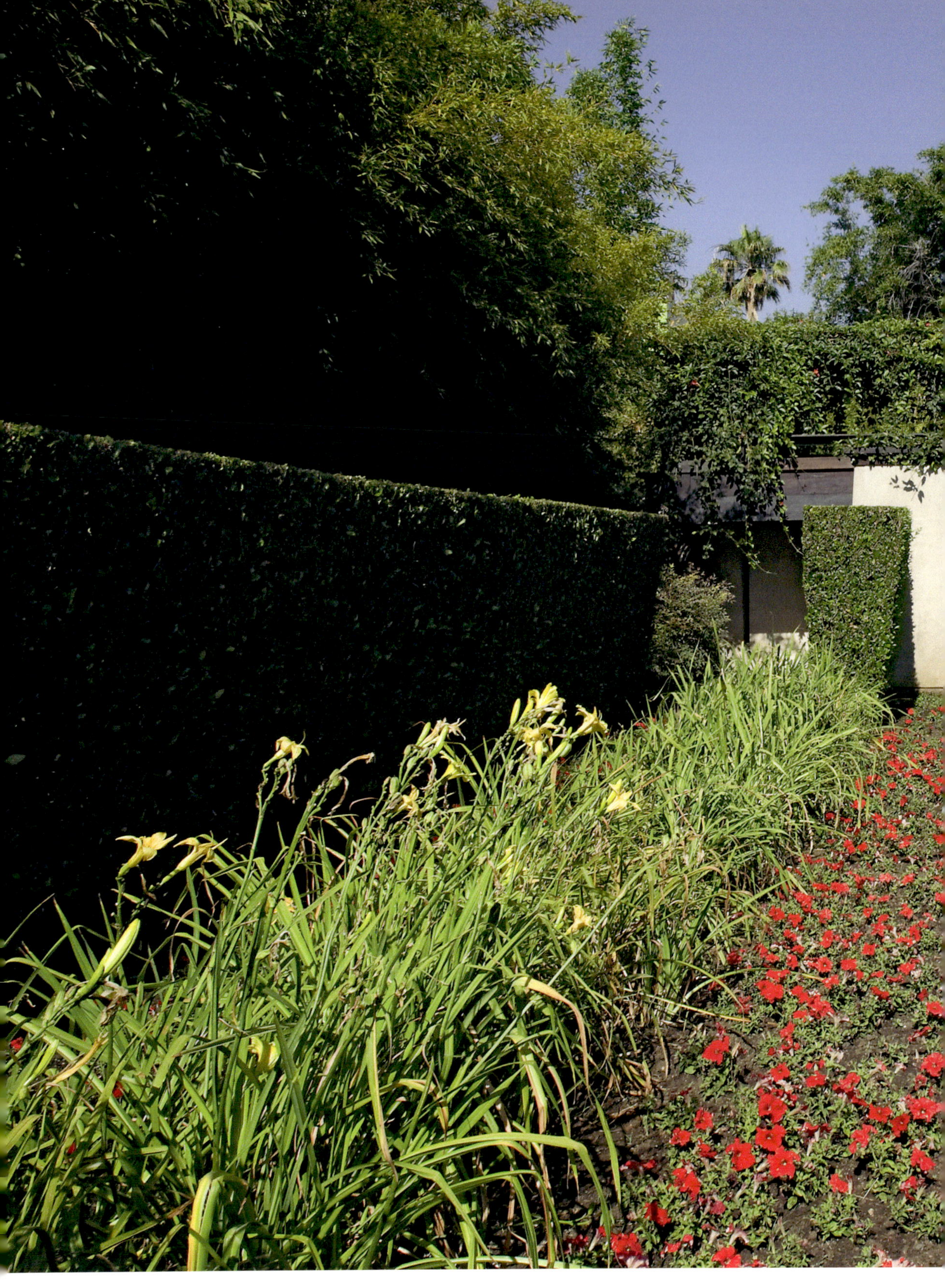

PLATE 3 Front garden, looking west.

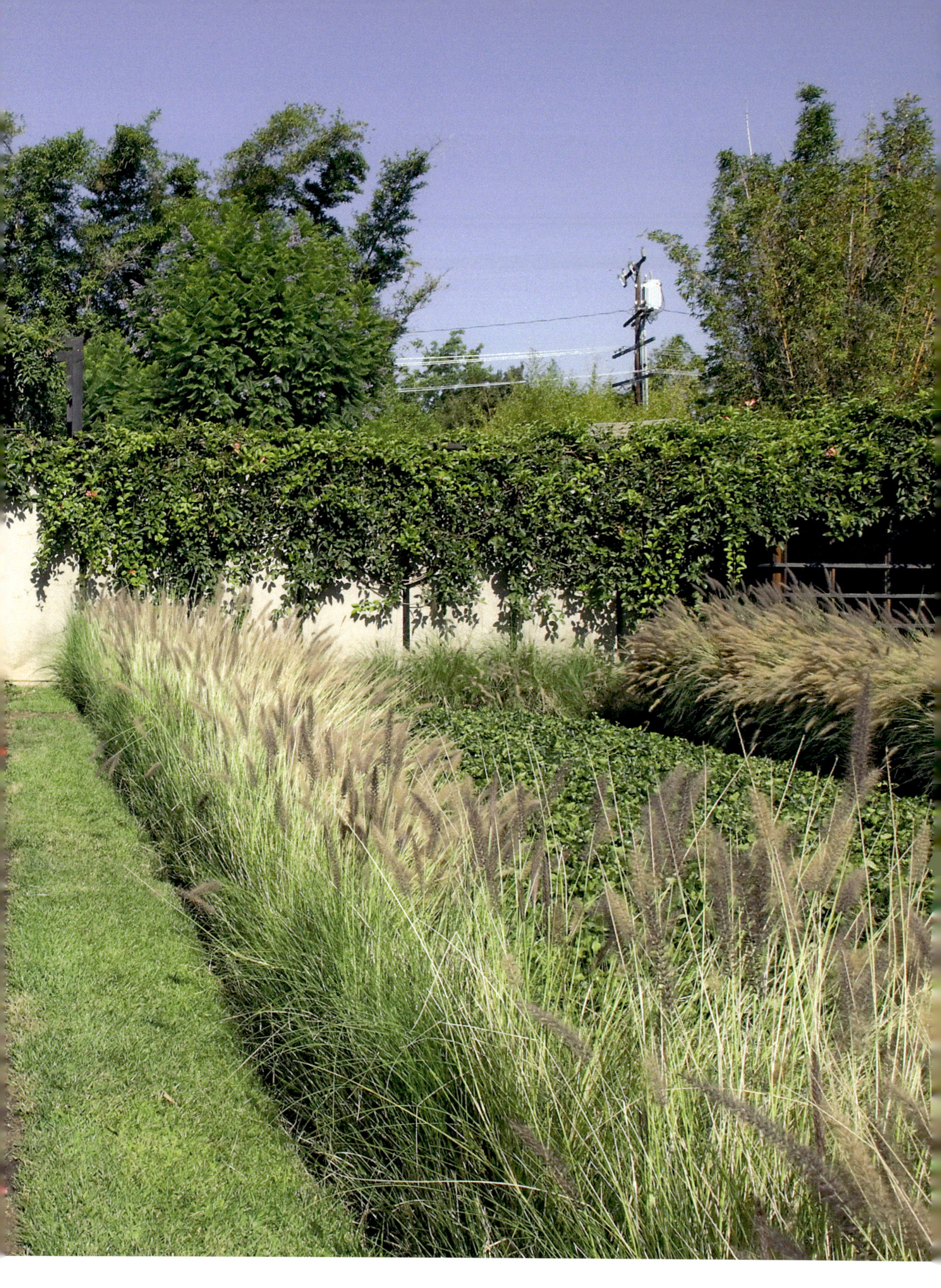

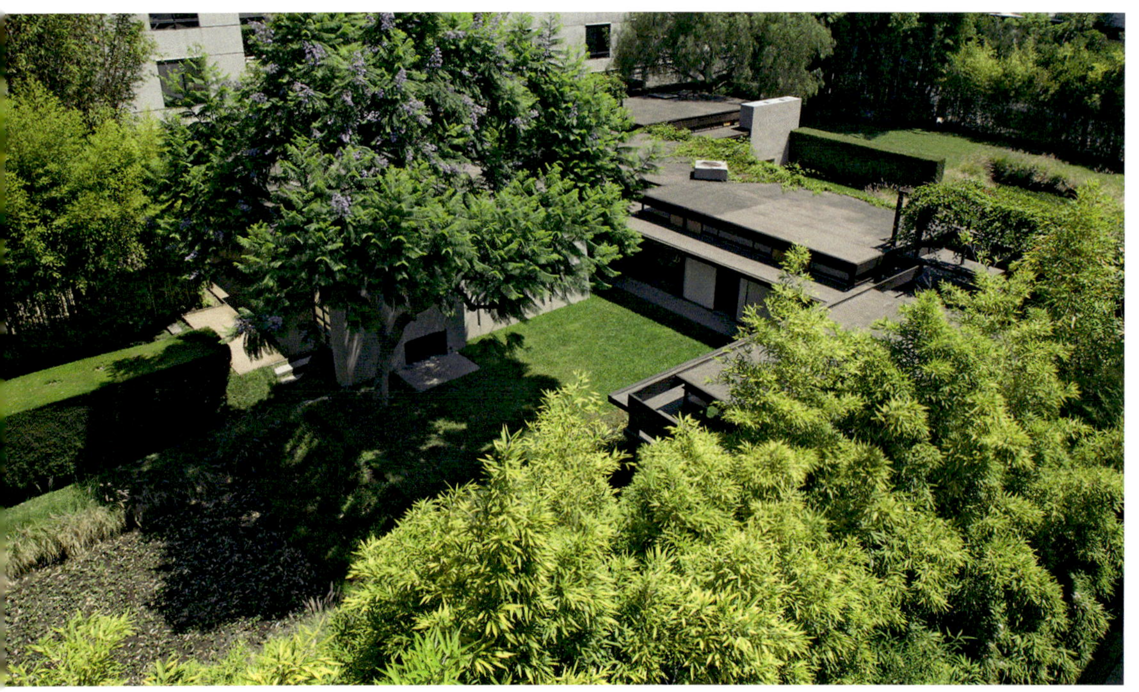

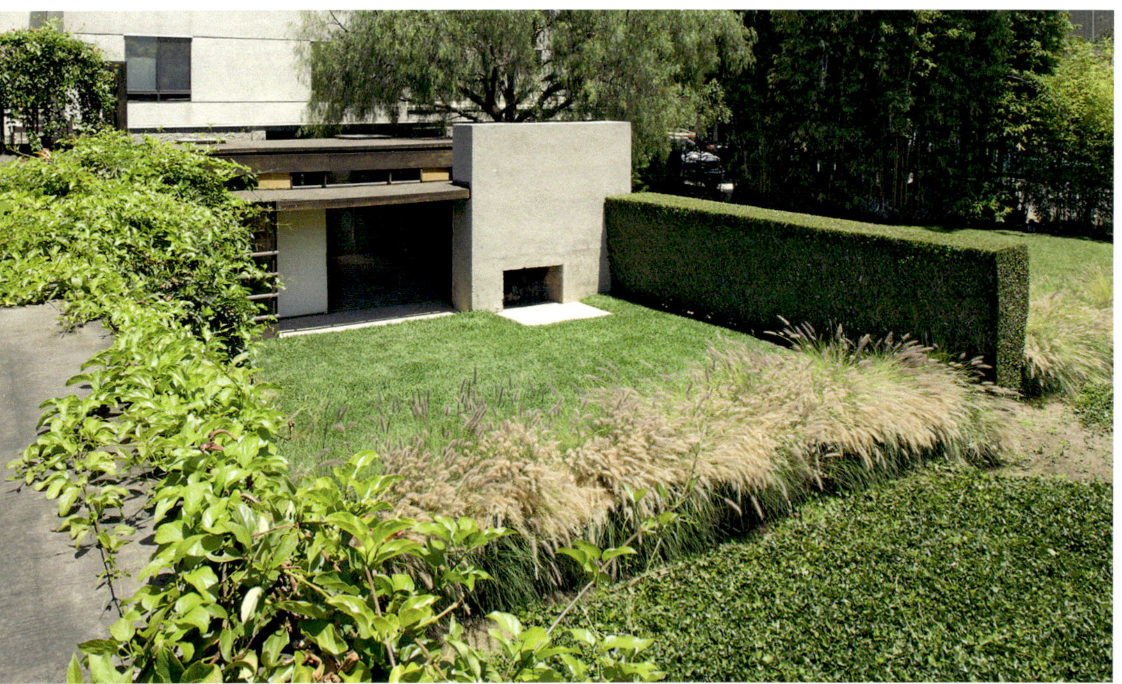

PLATE 4 House and garden from above, looking northeast.

PLATE 5 Chace patio, looking northeast from the Schindler sleeping basket.

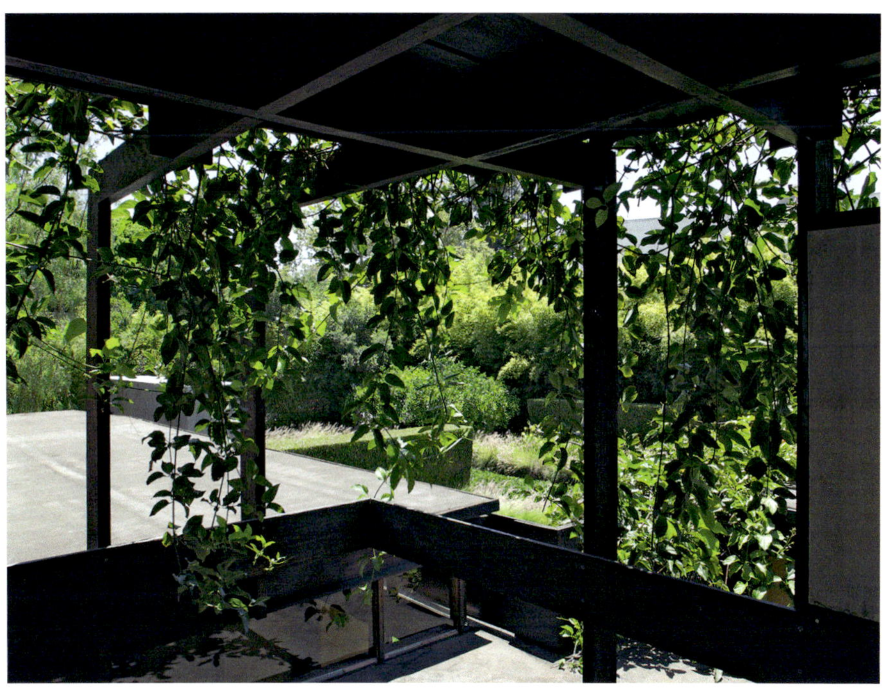

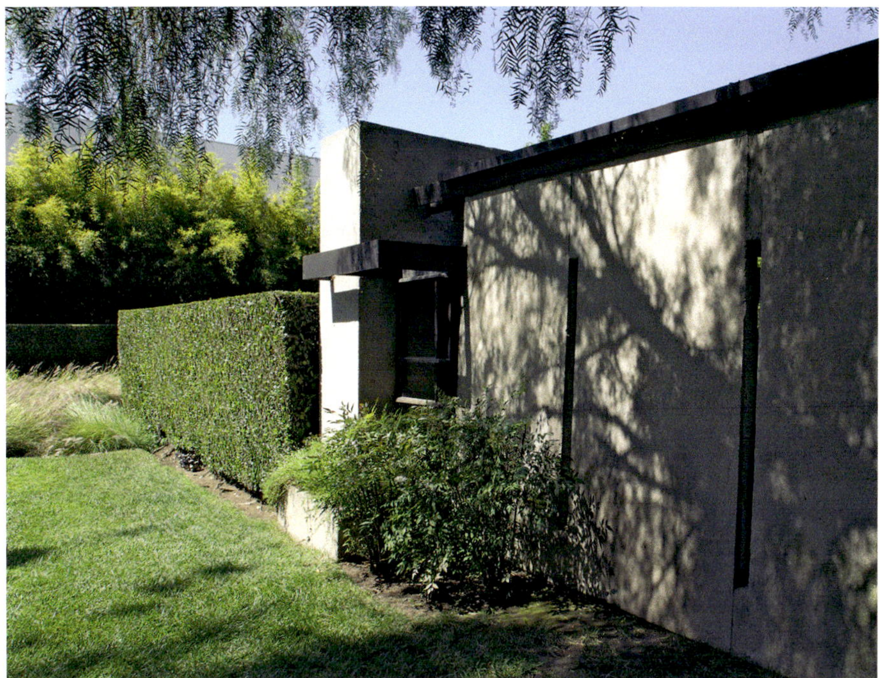

PLATE 6 Chace sleeping basket, looking southeast.

PLATE 7 East elevation, C.B.C. studio.

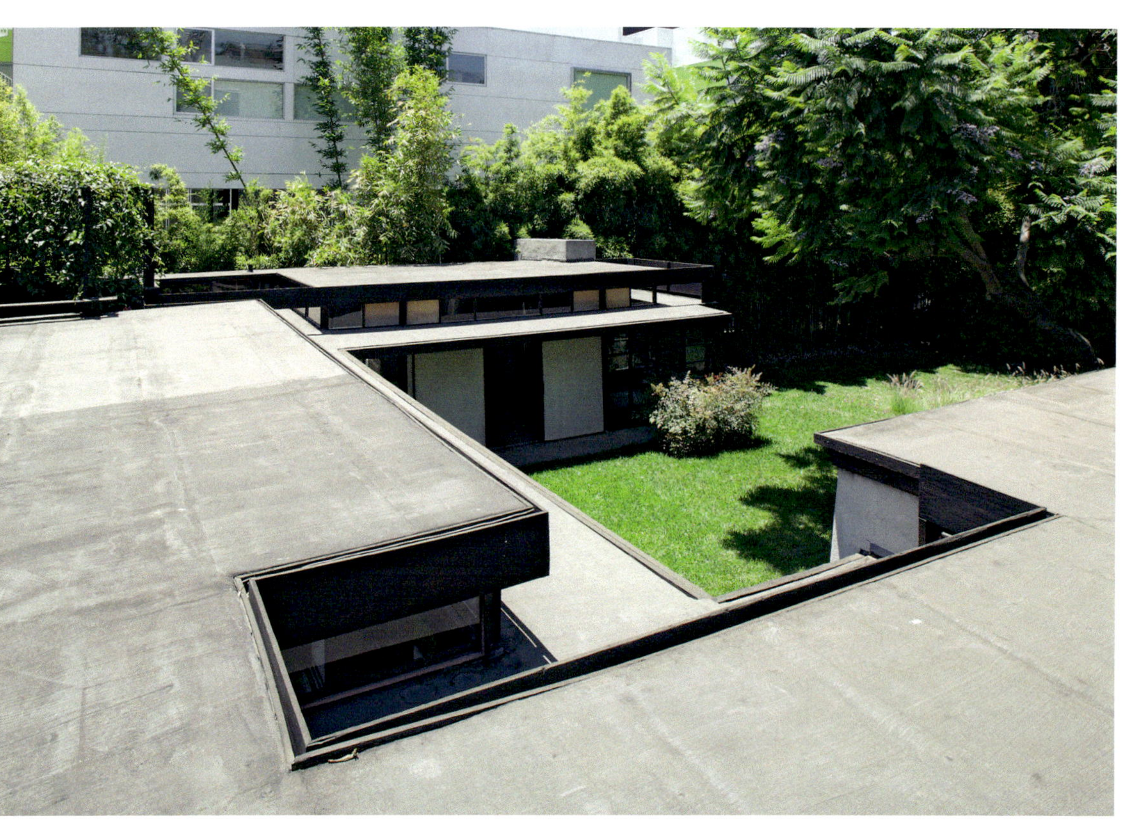

PLATE 8 Schindler patio from above, looking southwest.

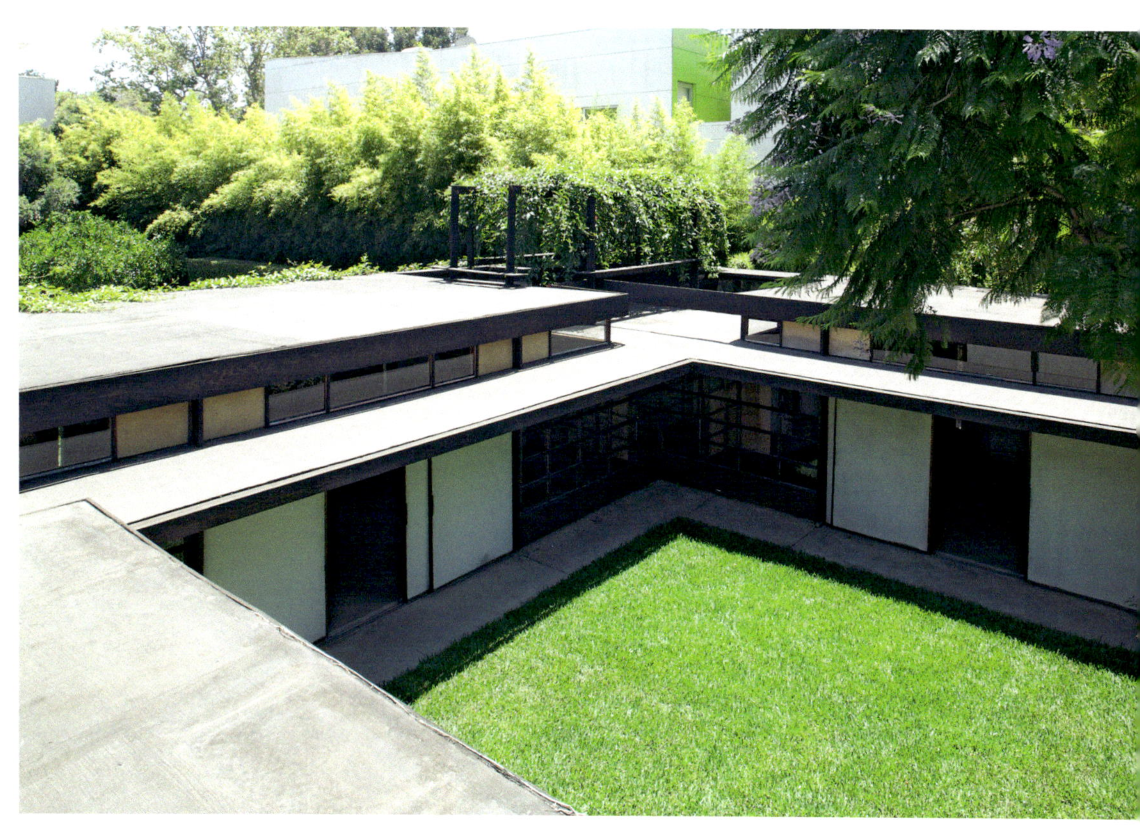

PLATE 9 Schindler patio from above, looking southeast.

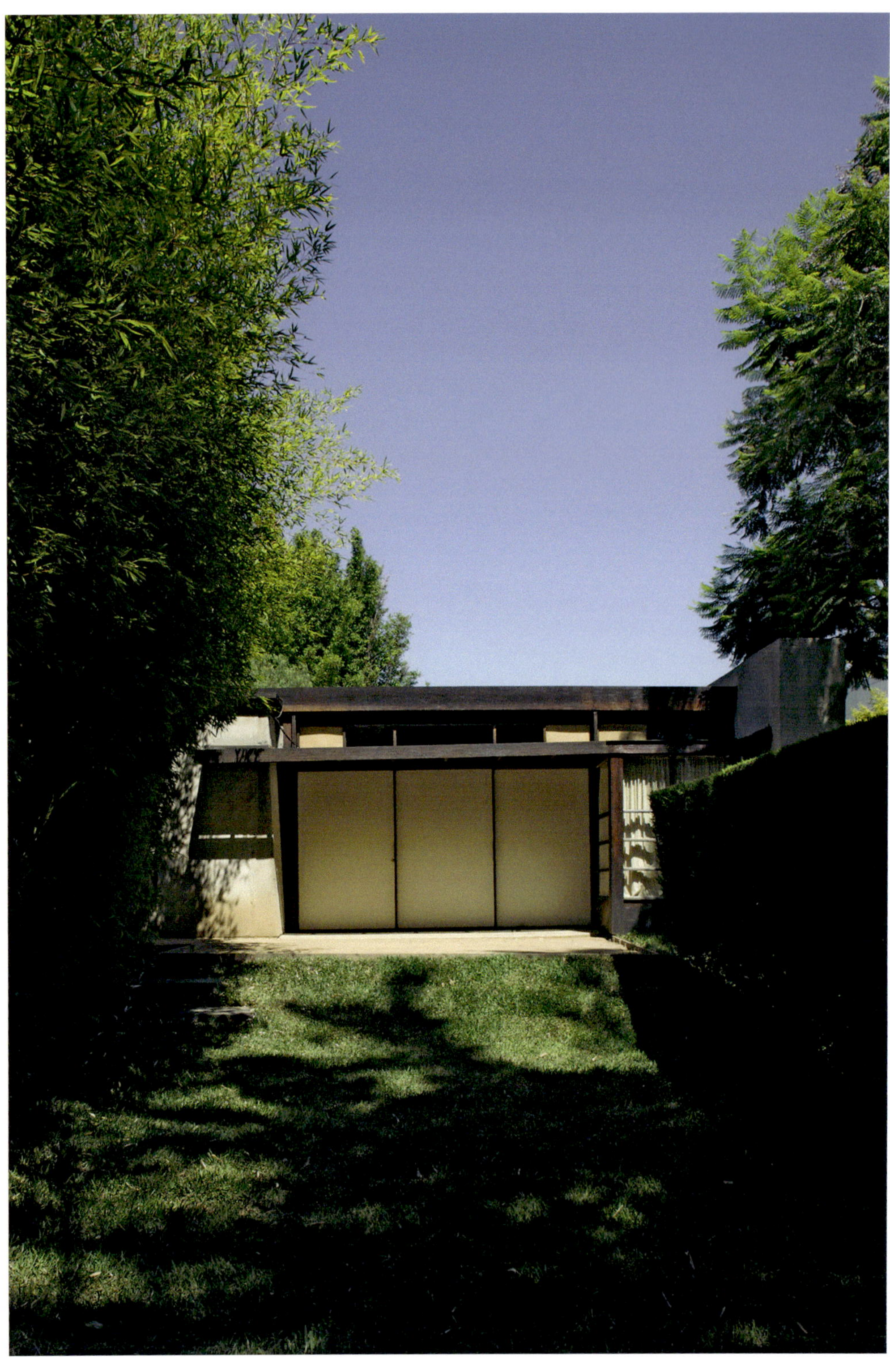

PLATE 10 Guest apartment west elevation.

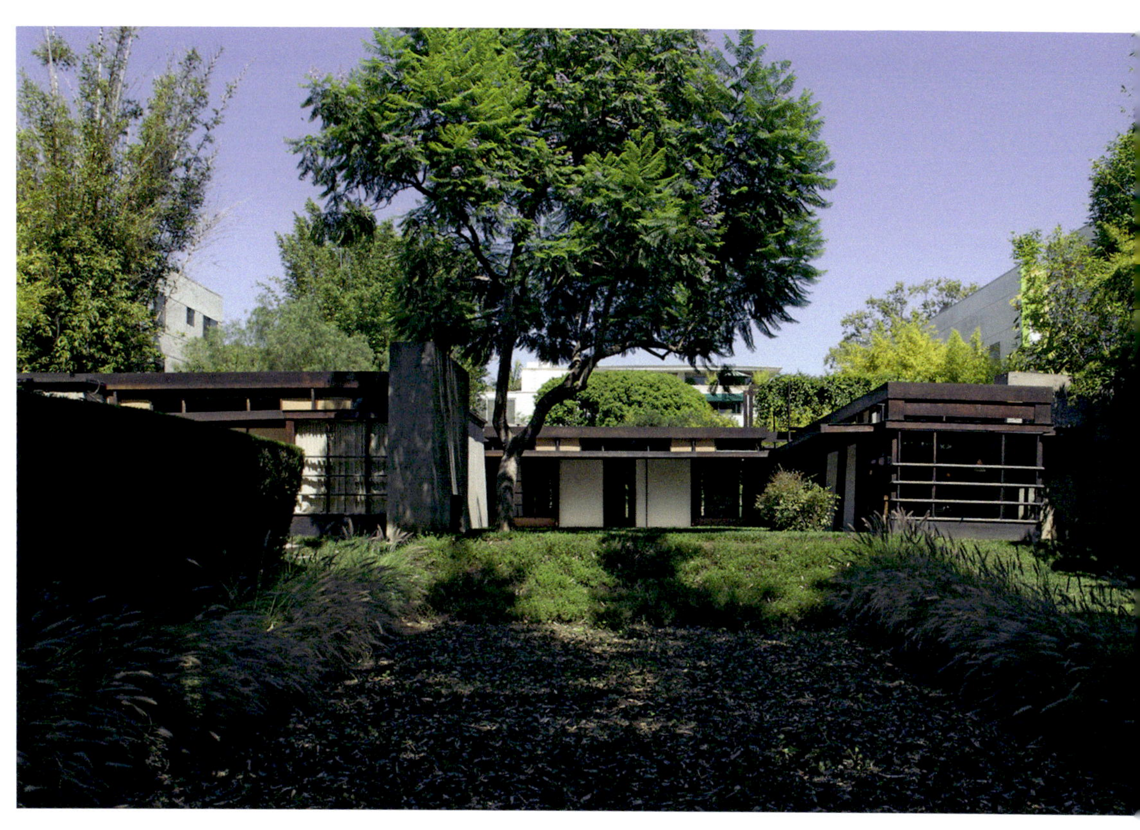

PLATE 11 West elevation.

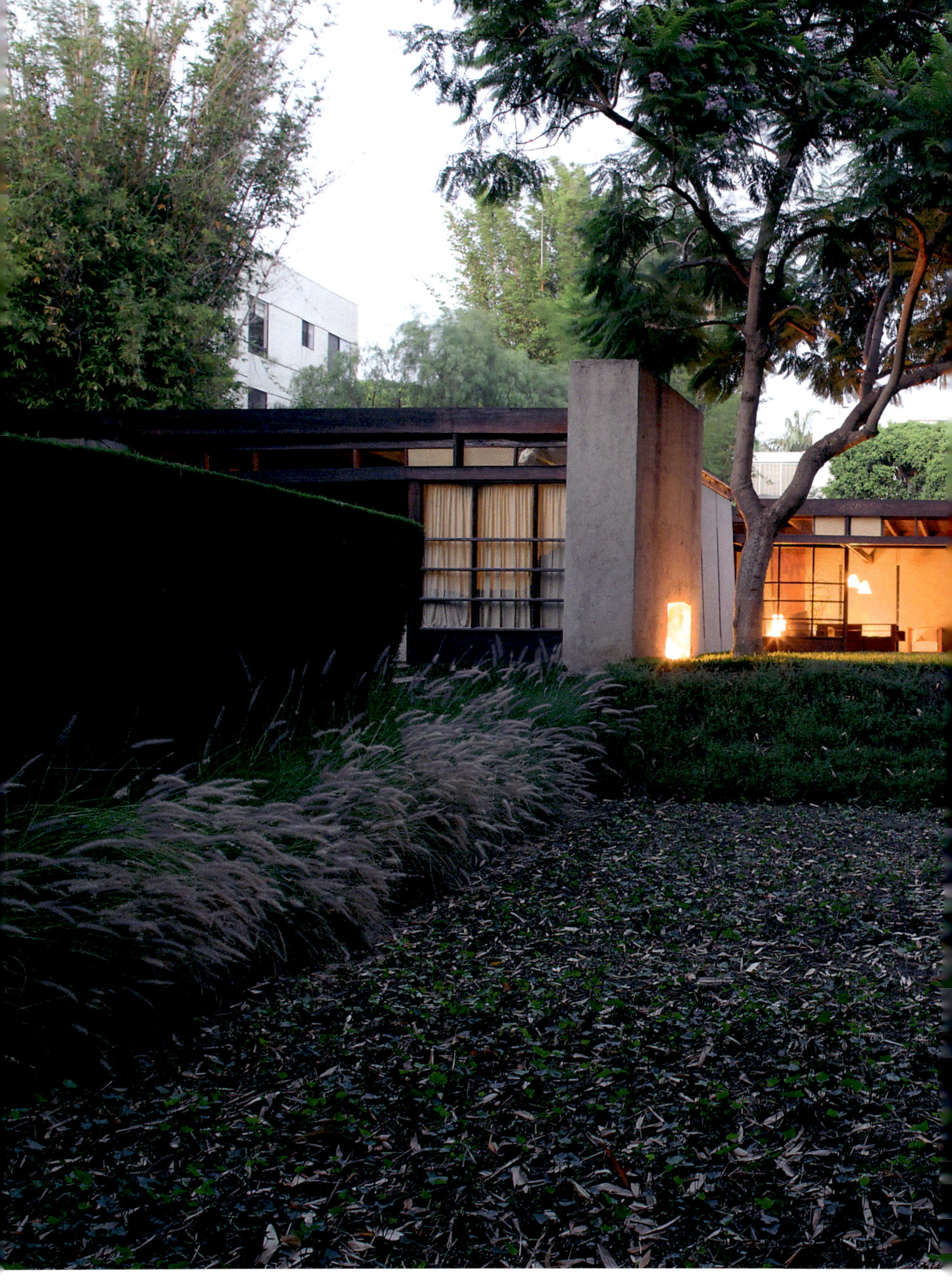

PLATE 12 West elevation.

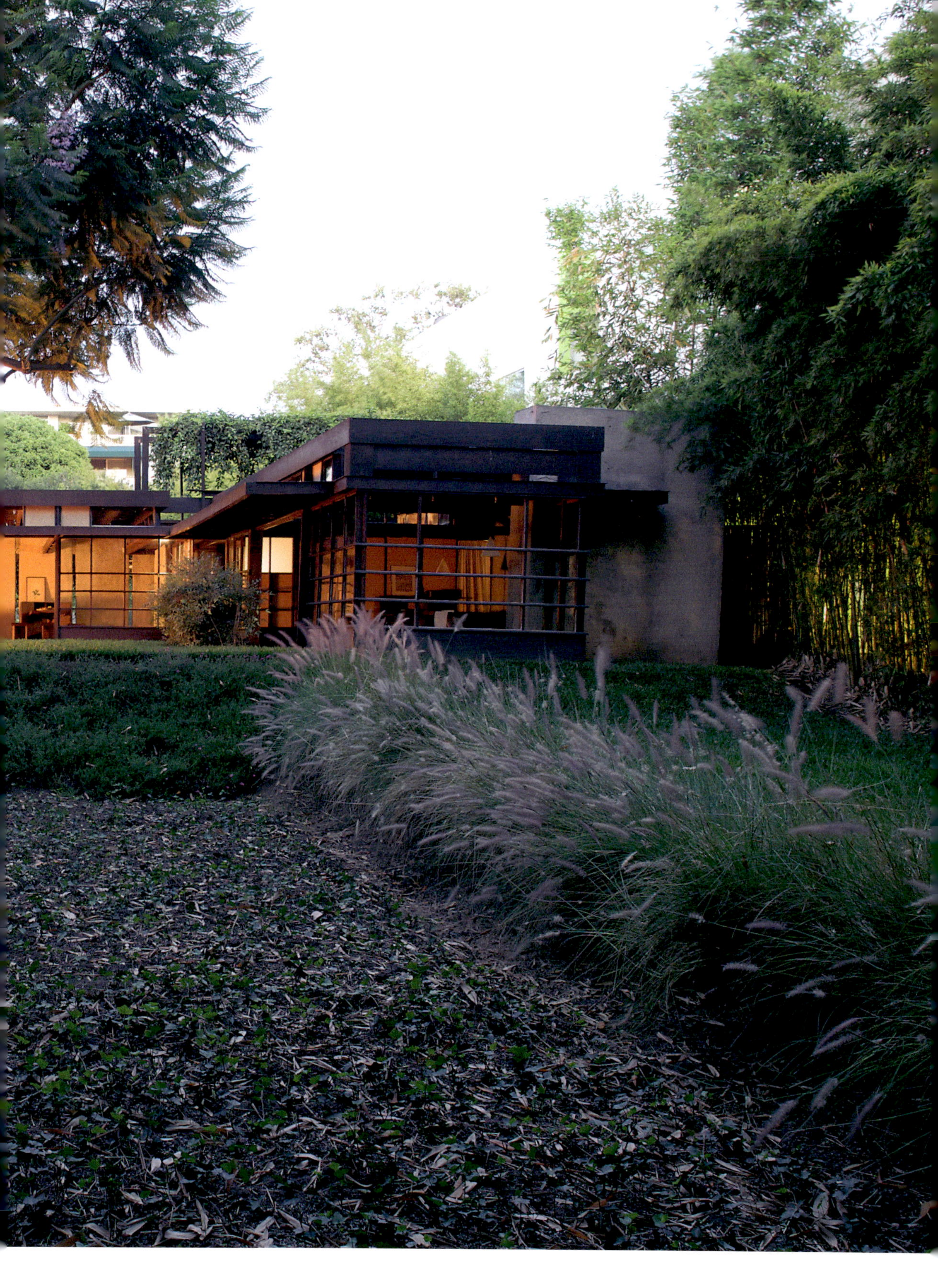

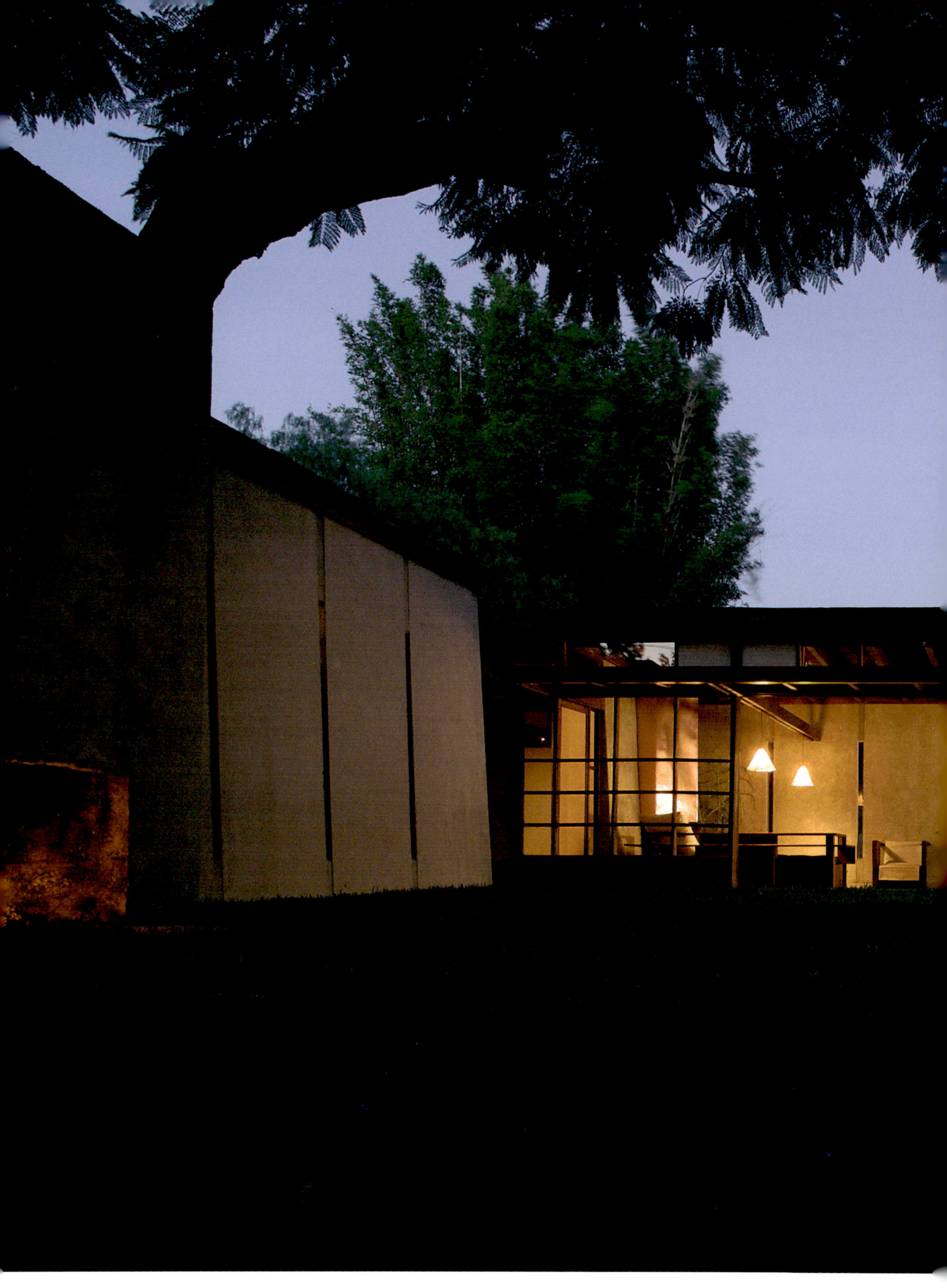

PLATE 13 West elevation.

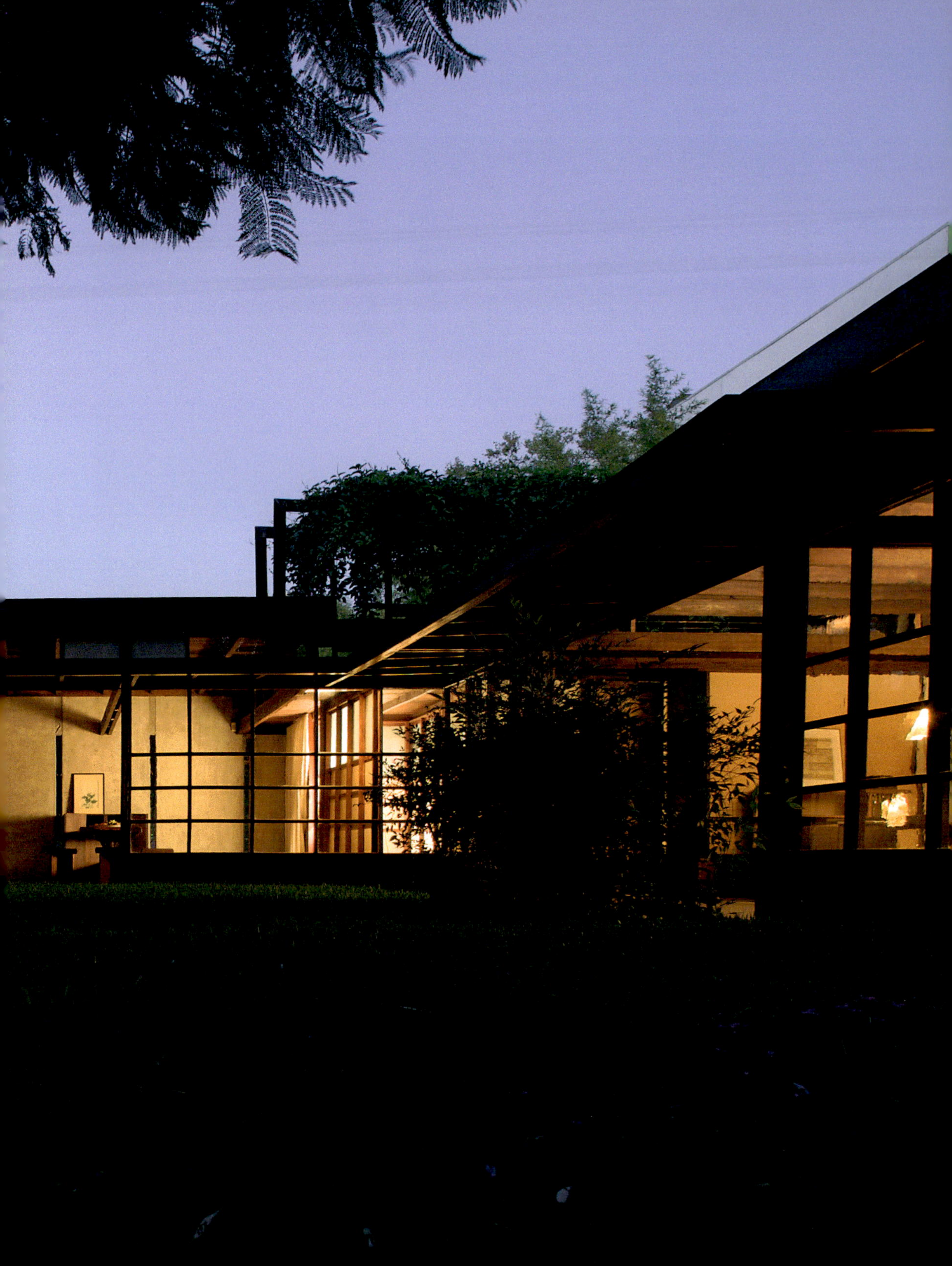

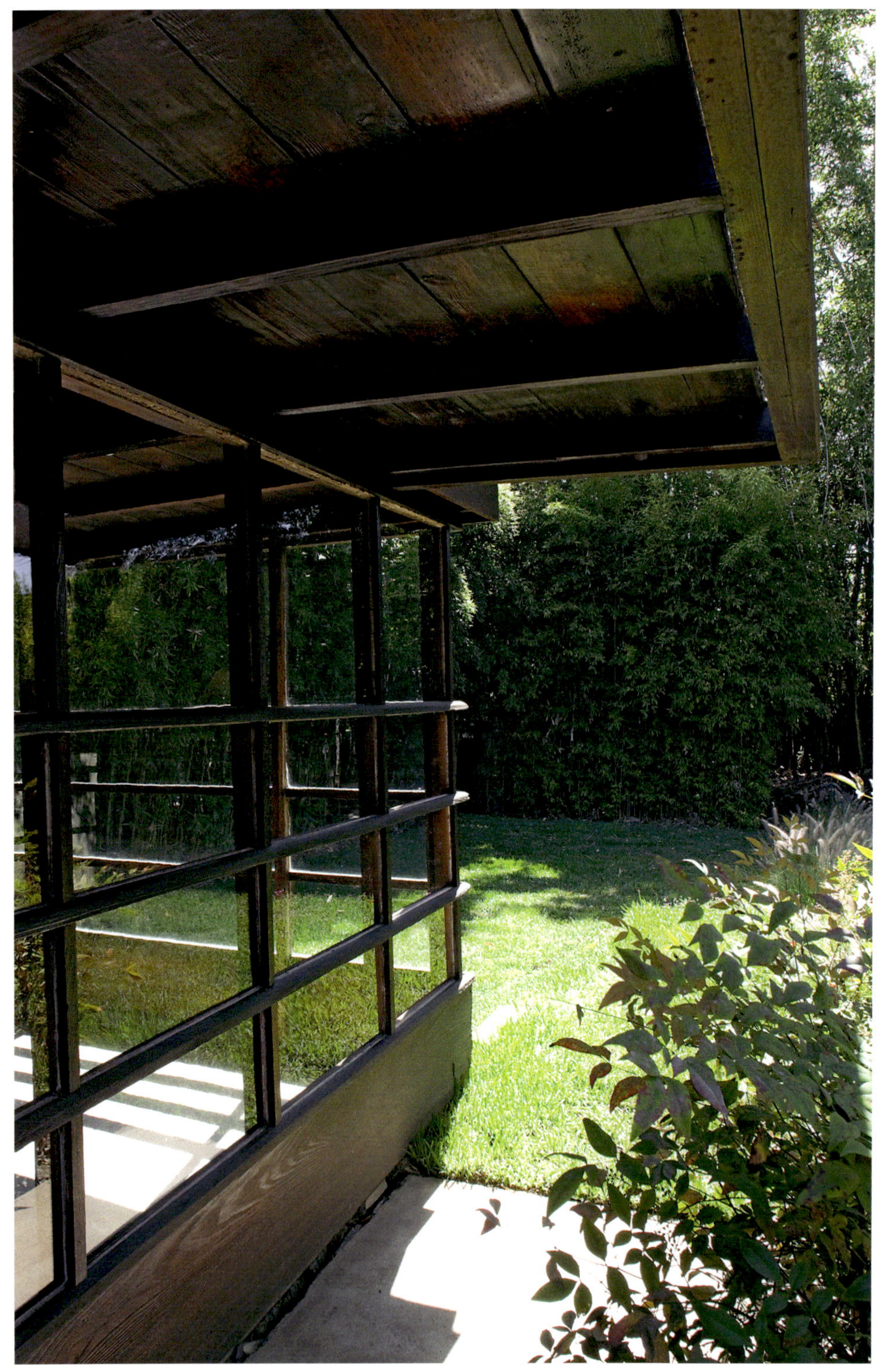

PLATE 14 R. M. S. studio, looking west.

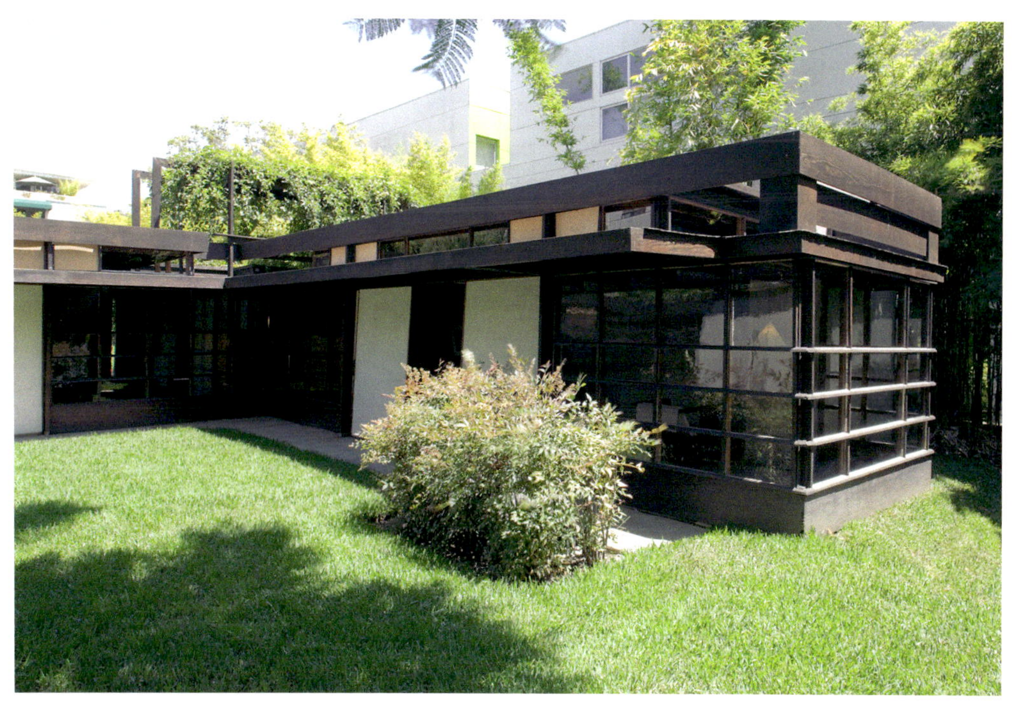

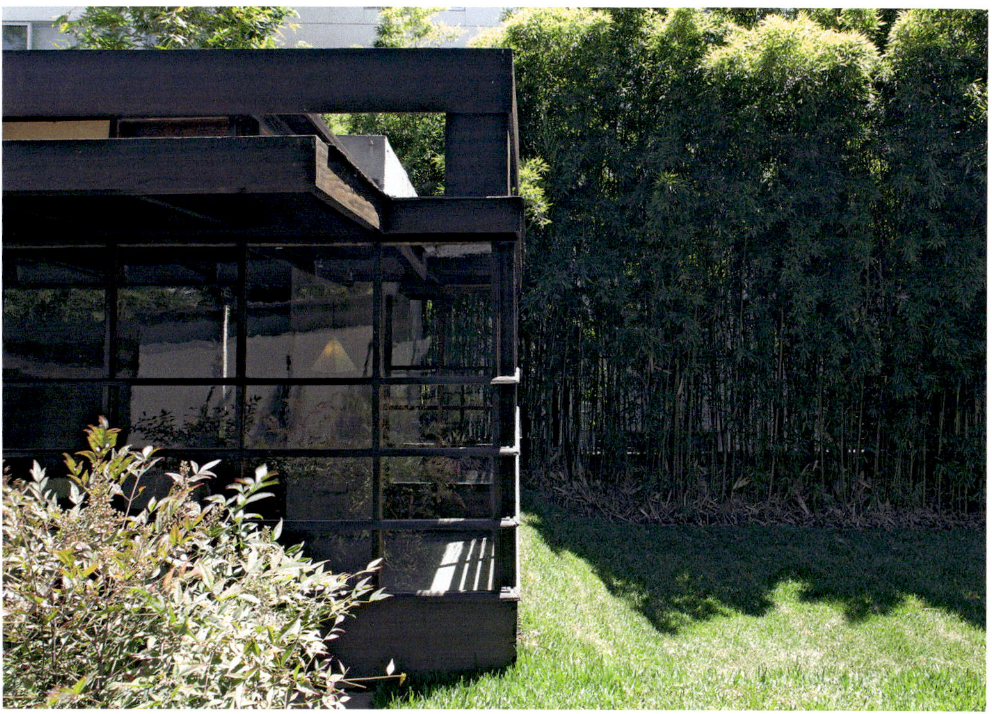

PLATE 15 R.M.S. studio, looking southeast.

PLATE 16 R.M.S. studio, looking south.

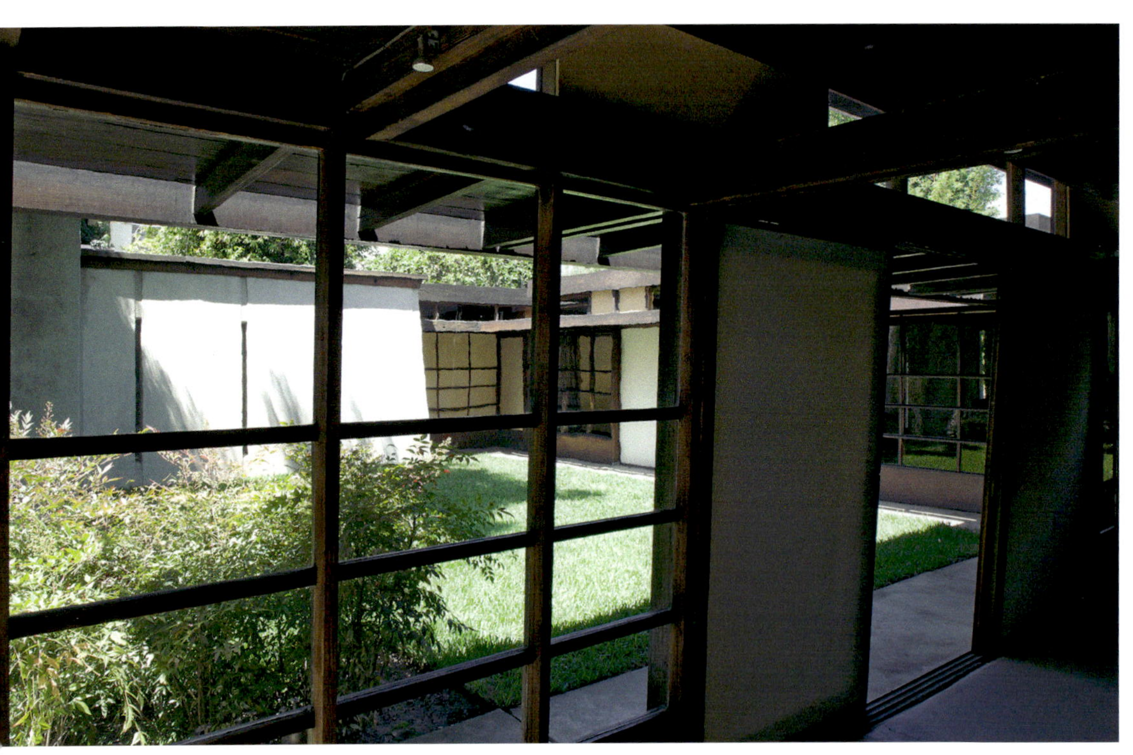

PLATE 17 Schindler patio from the R. M. S. studio, looking northeast.

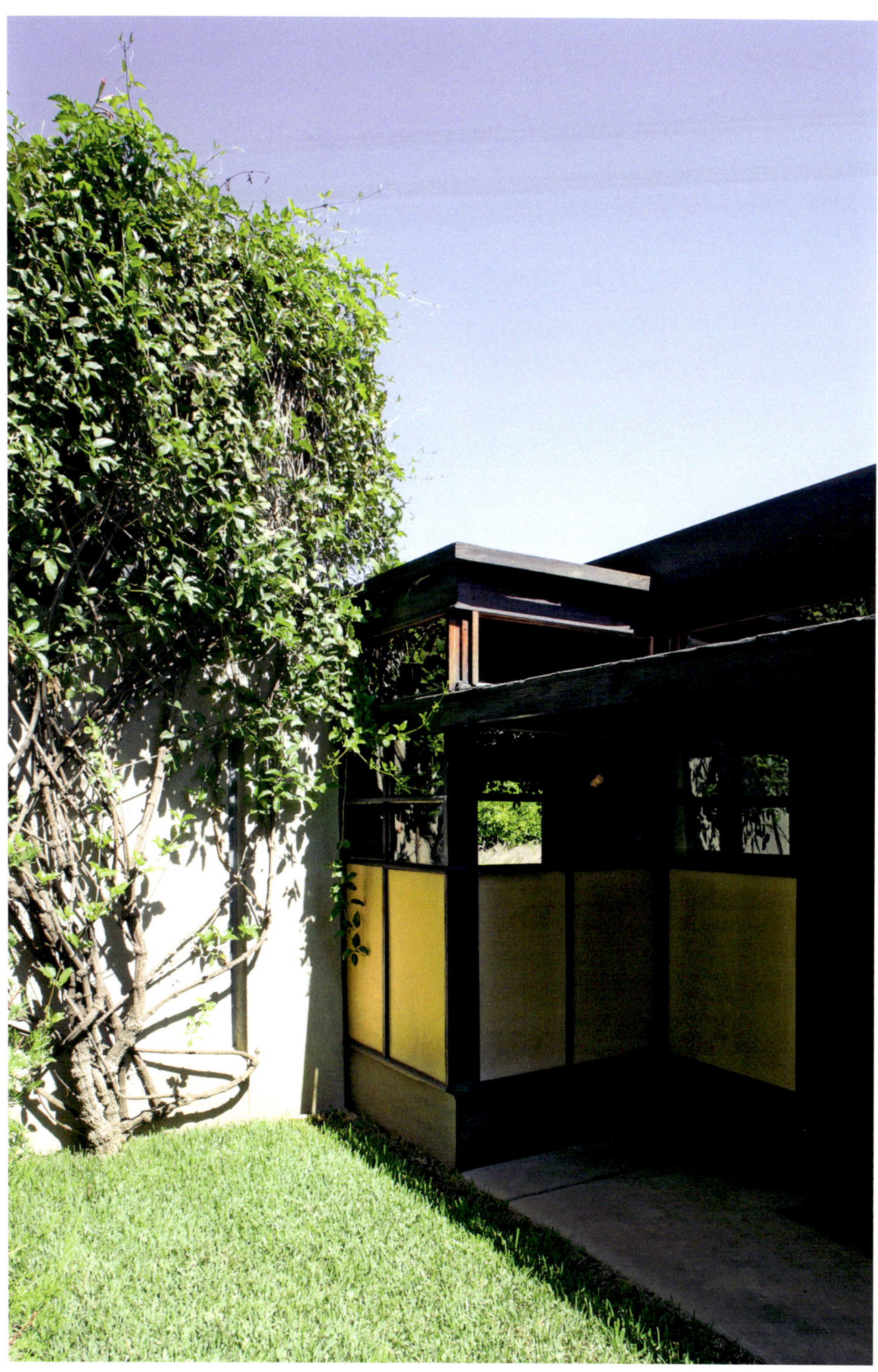

PLATE 18 Service yard, looking southeast.

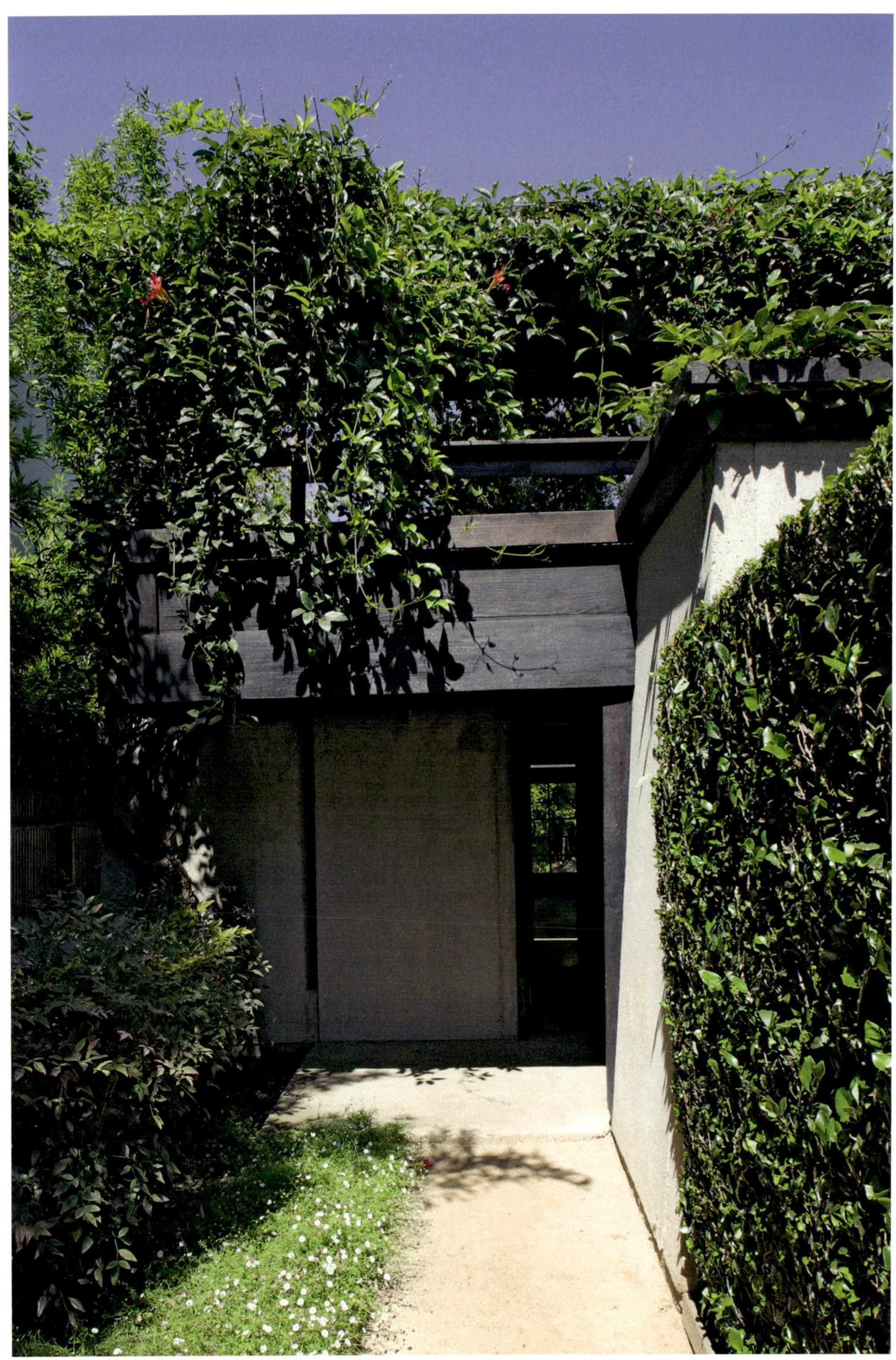

PLATE 19 Schindler entry.

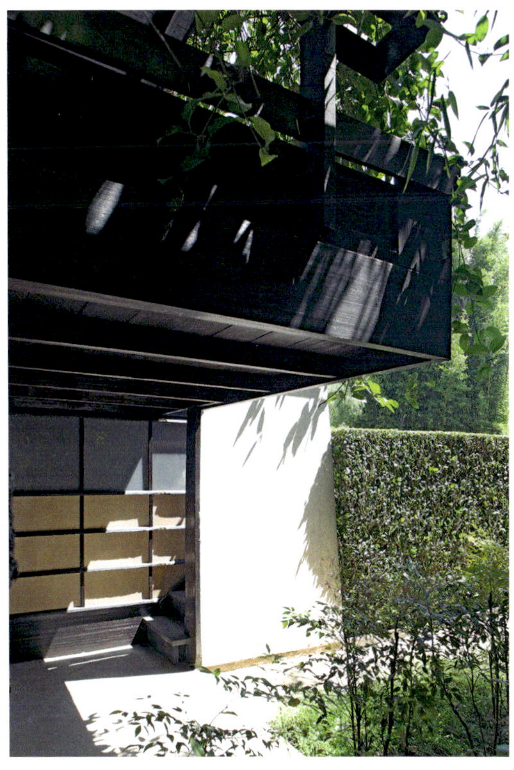

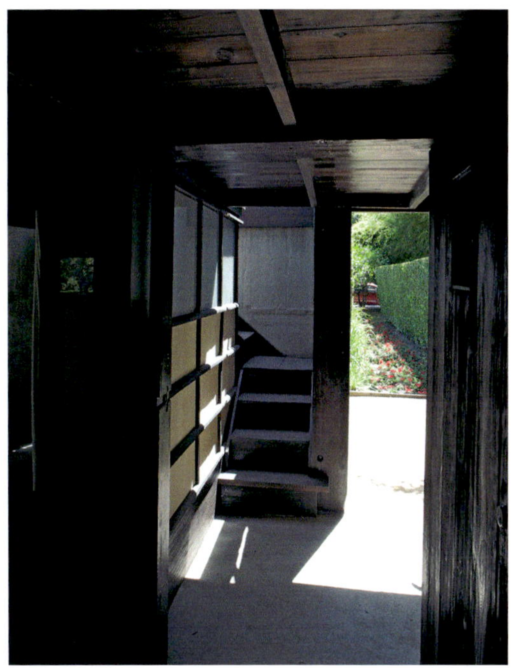

PLATE 20 Schindler entry, with sleeping basket above.

PLATE 21 Schindler entry, looking toward the front garden.

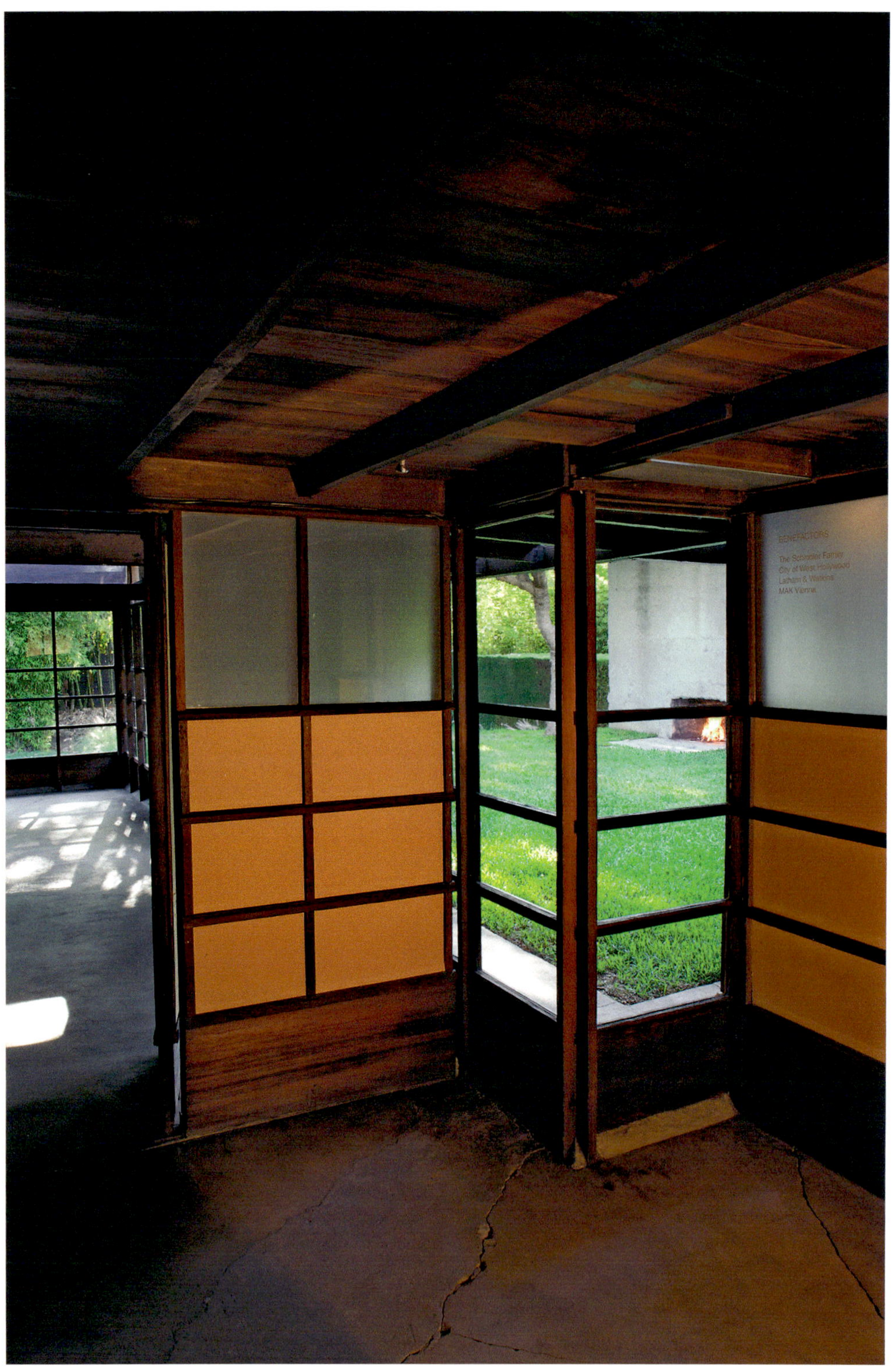

PLATE 22 Schindler entry.

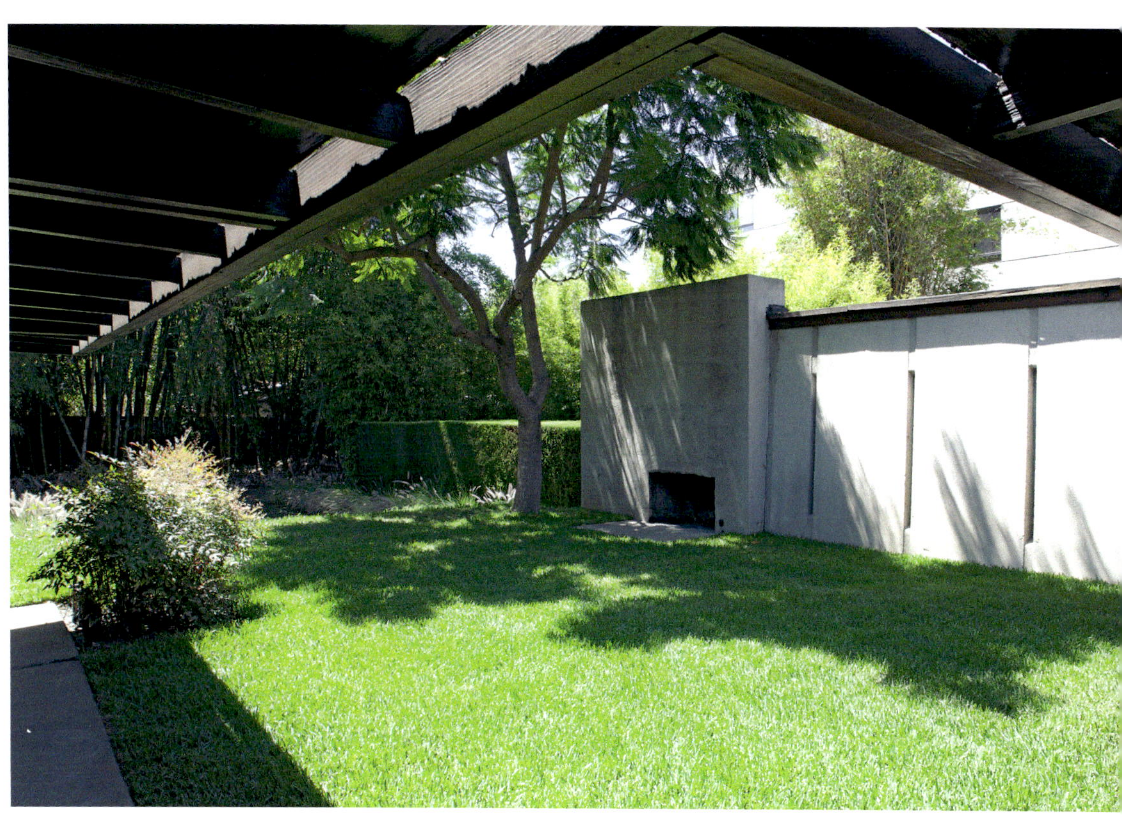

PLATE 23 Schindler patio, looking northwest.

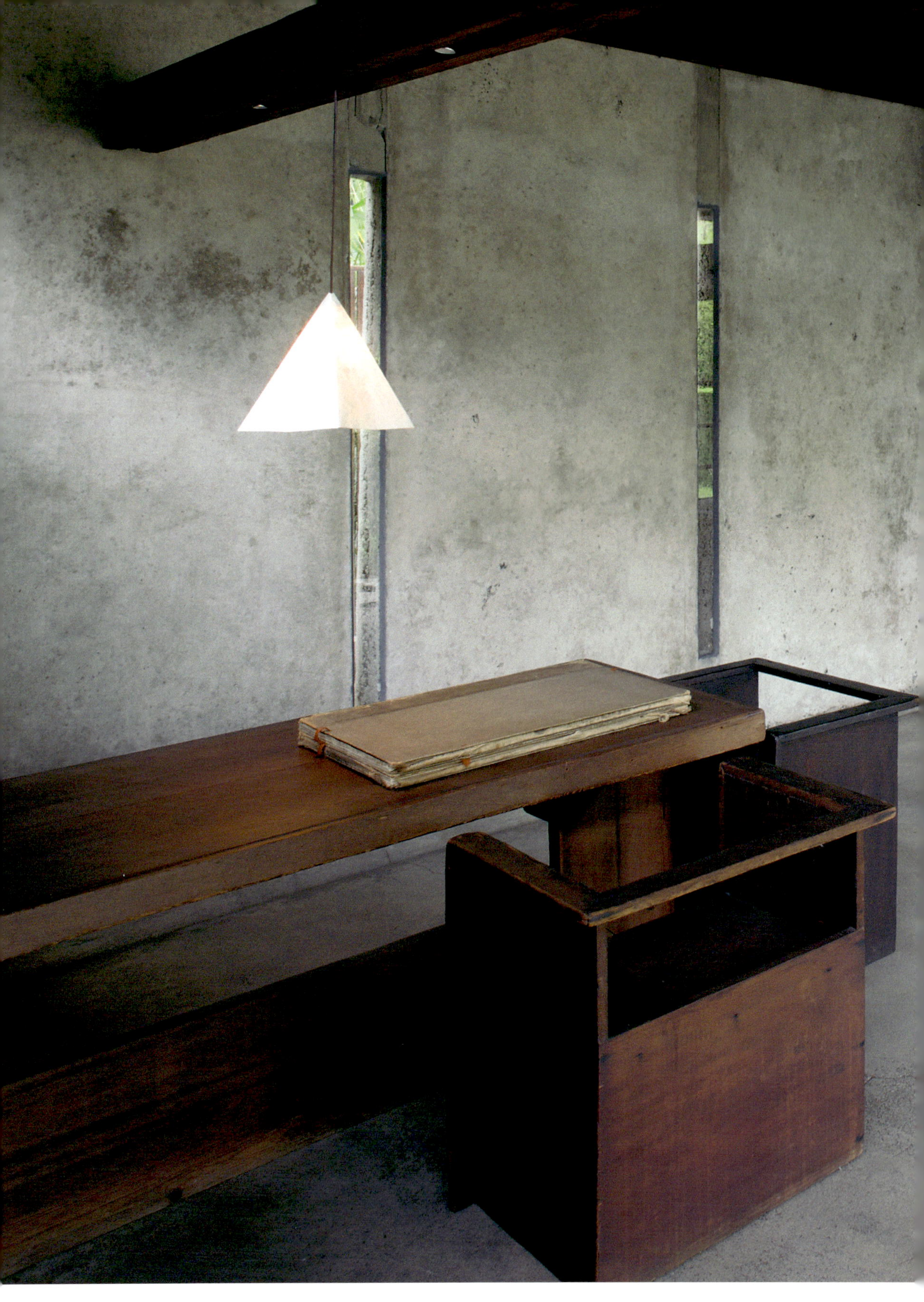

PLATE 24 R.M.S. studio.

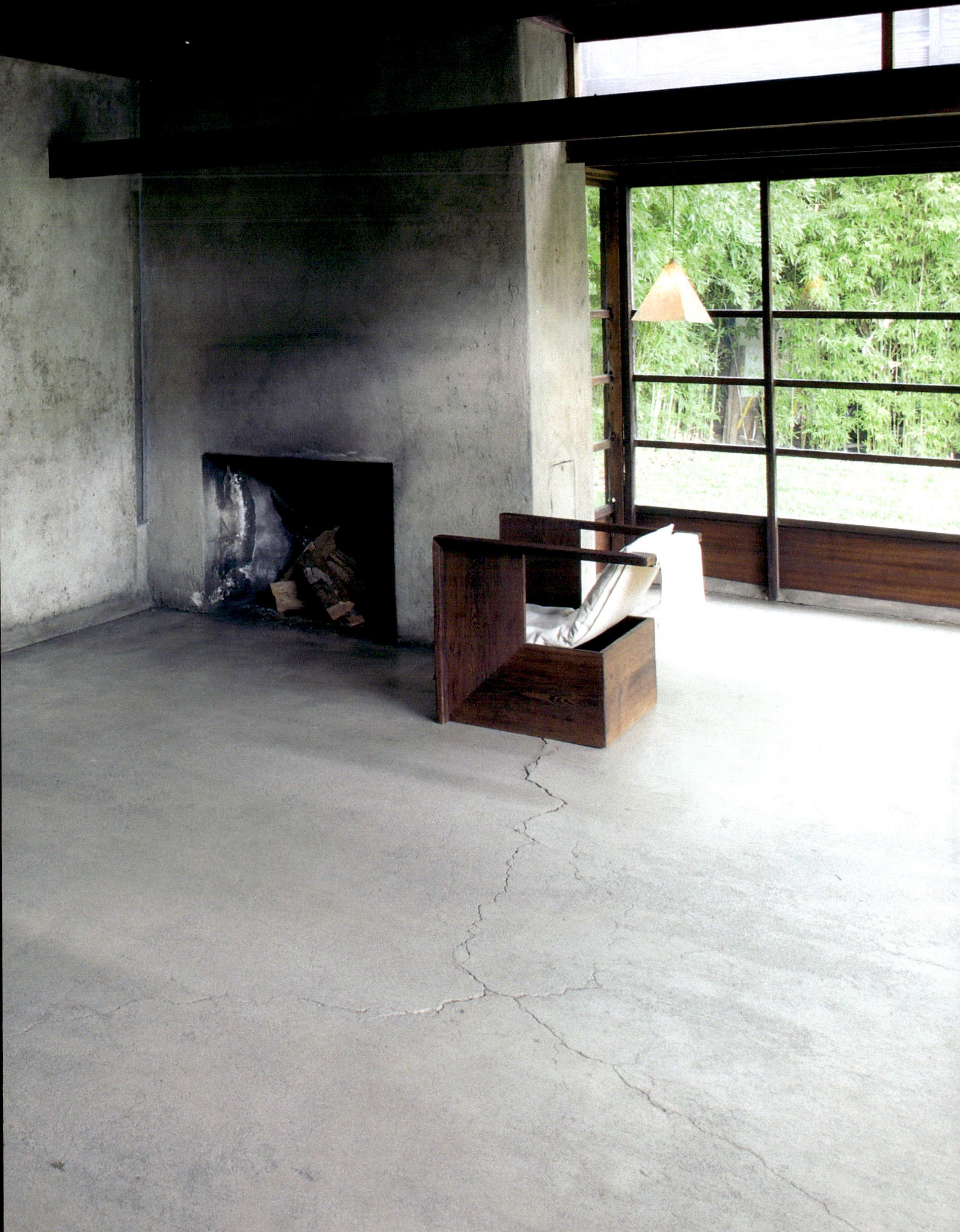

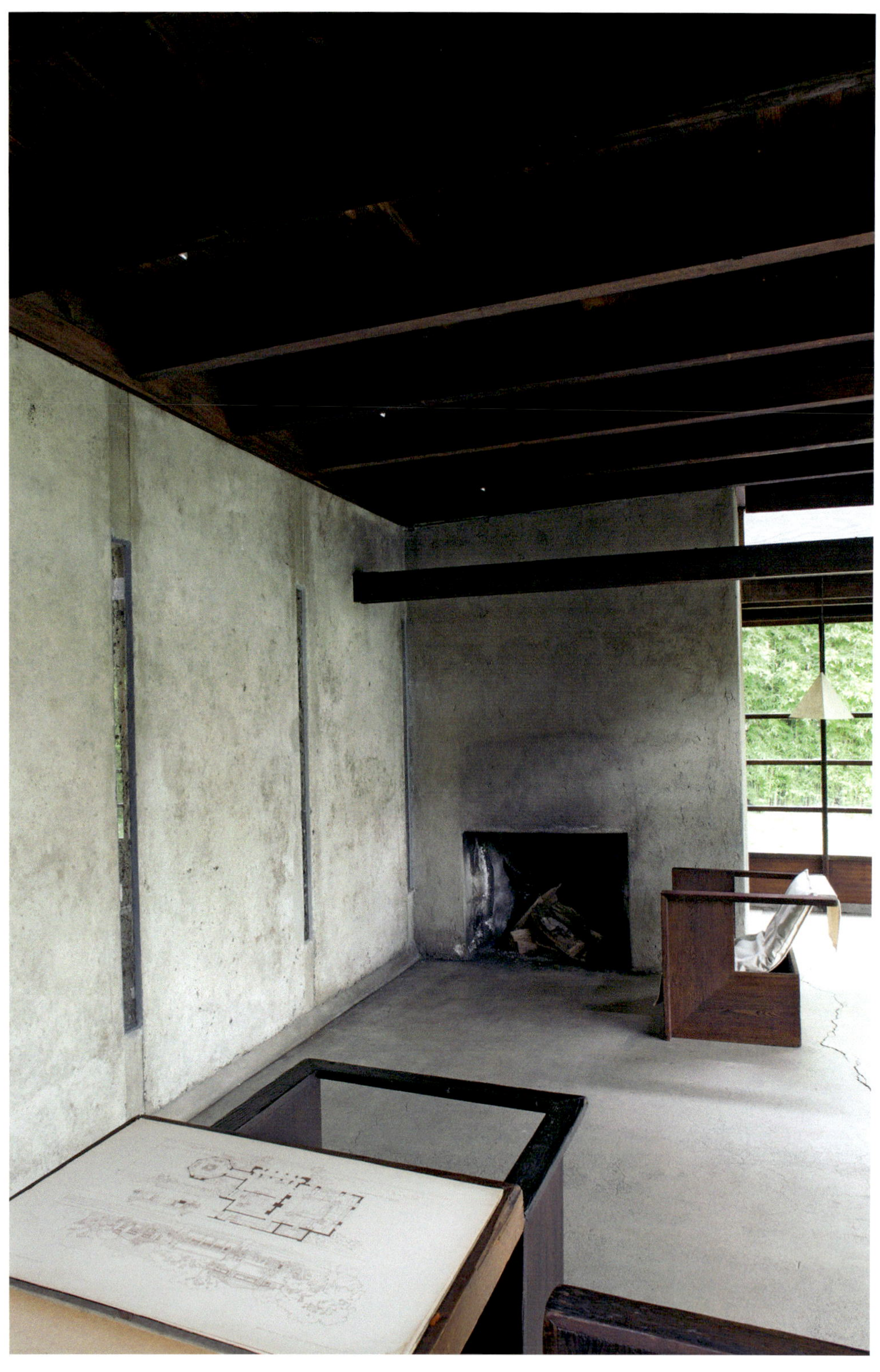

PLATE 25 R. M. S. studio. A copy of *Ausgeführte Bauten und Entwürfe von Frank Lloyd Wright,* frequently cited as a catalyst for Schindler's move to America, rests on the table.

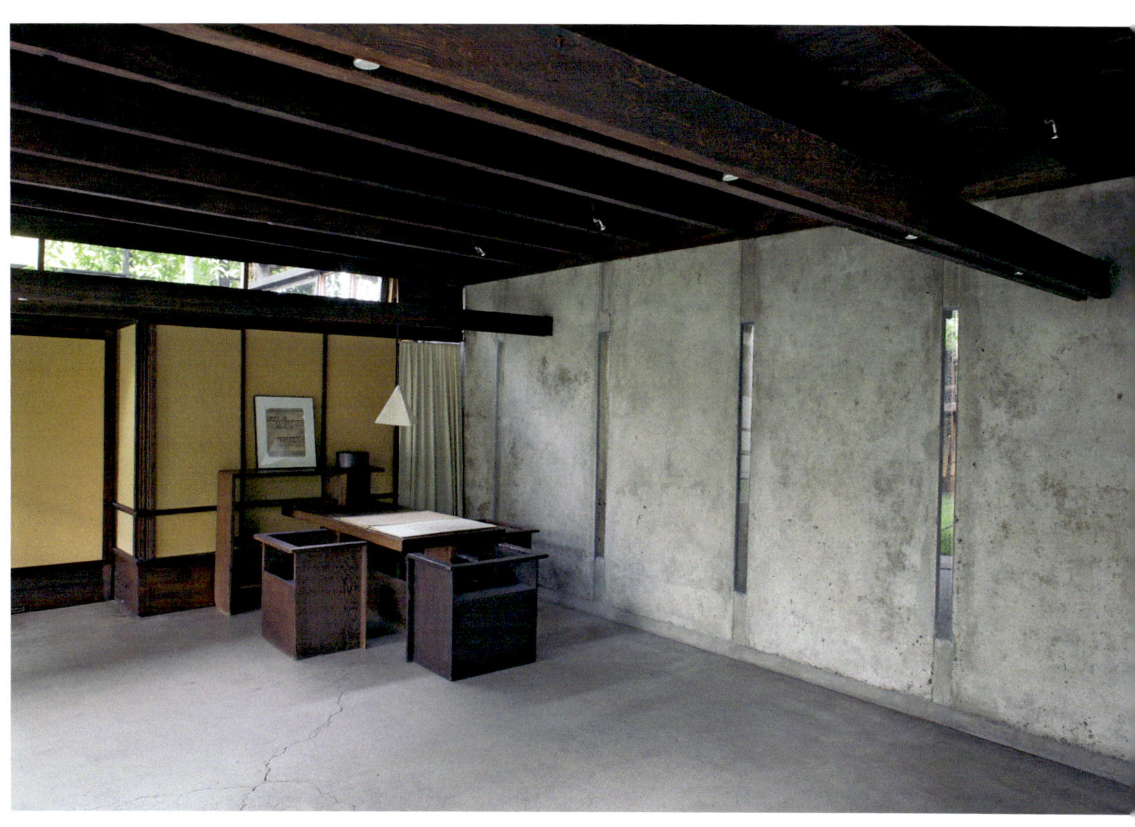

PLATE 26 R.M.S. studio.

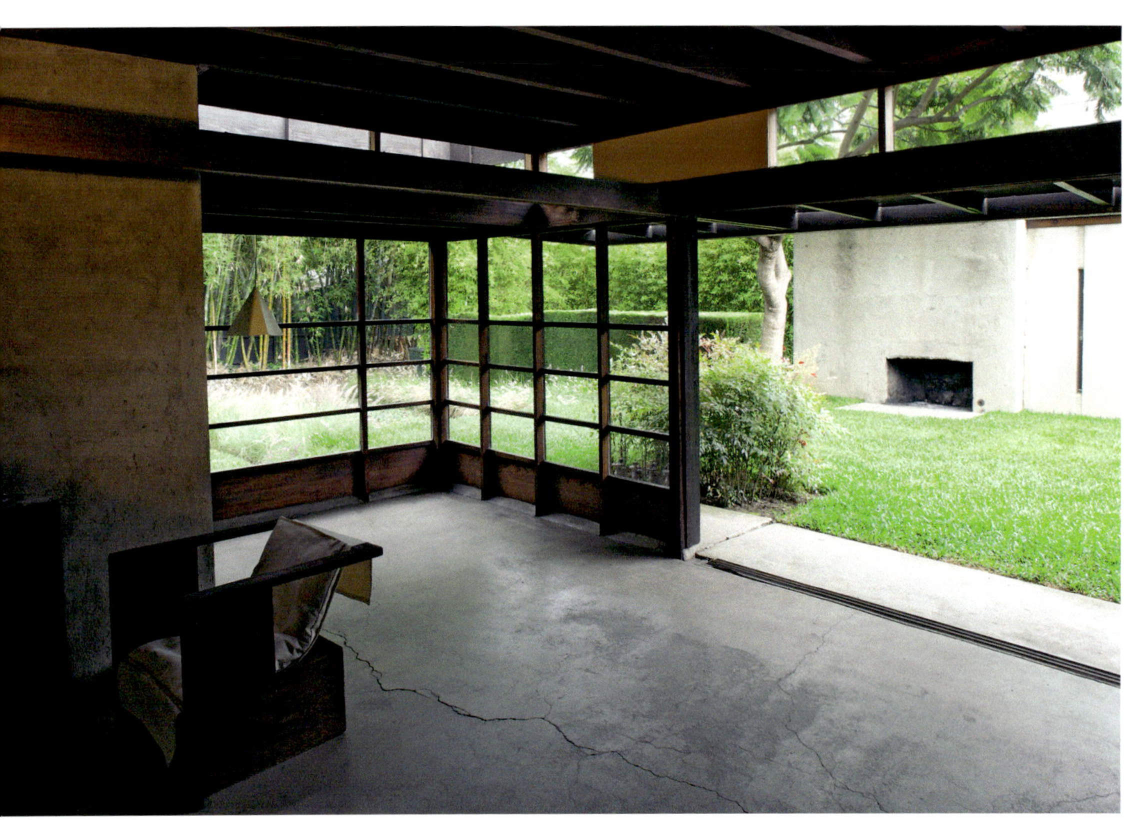

PLATE 27 R.M.S. studio.

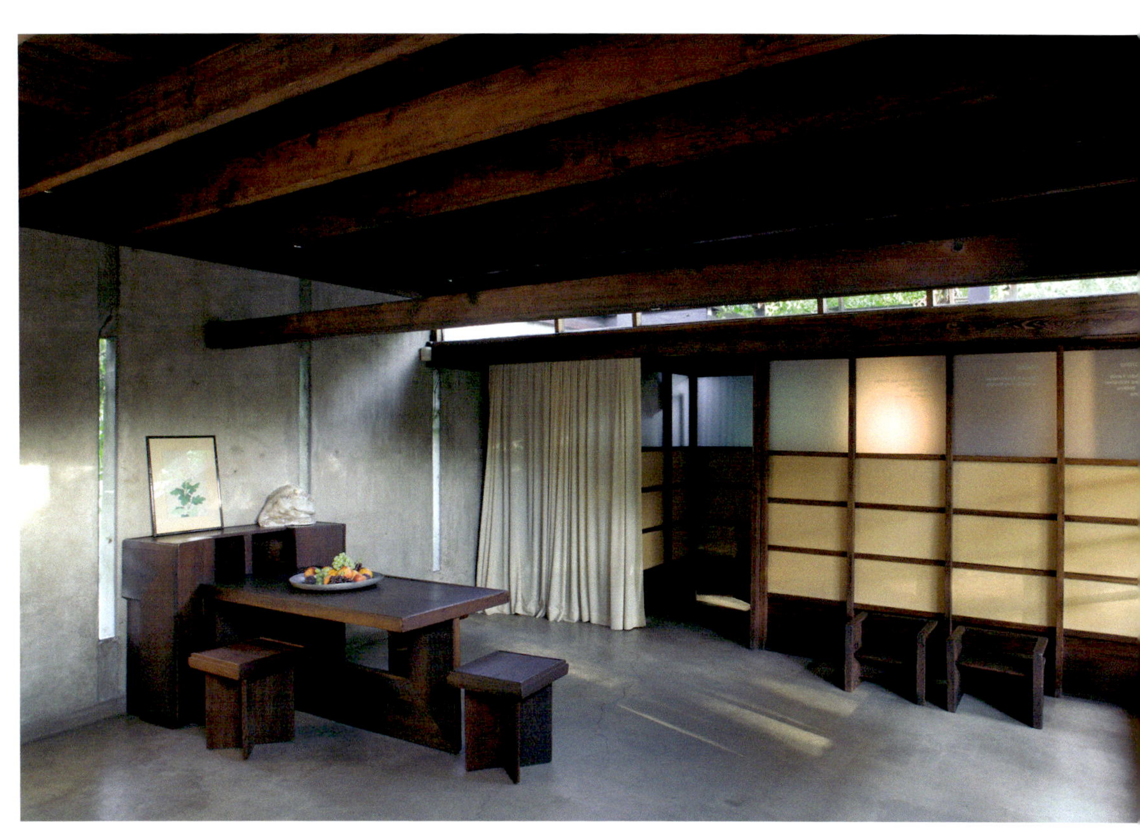

PLATE 28 S. P. G. studio.

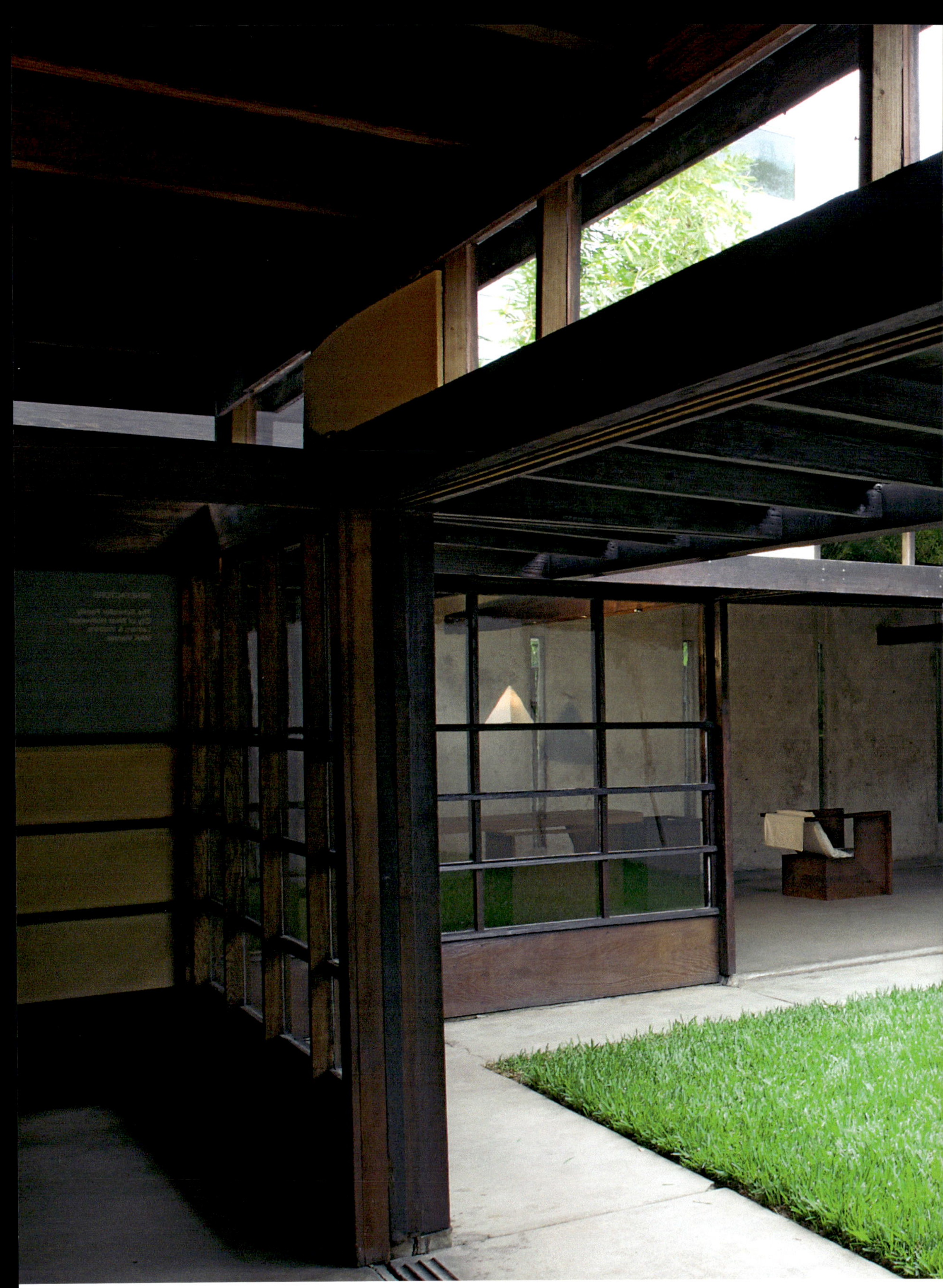

PLATE 29 Schindler patio.

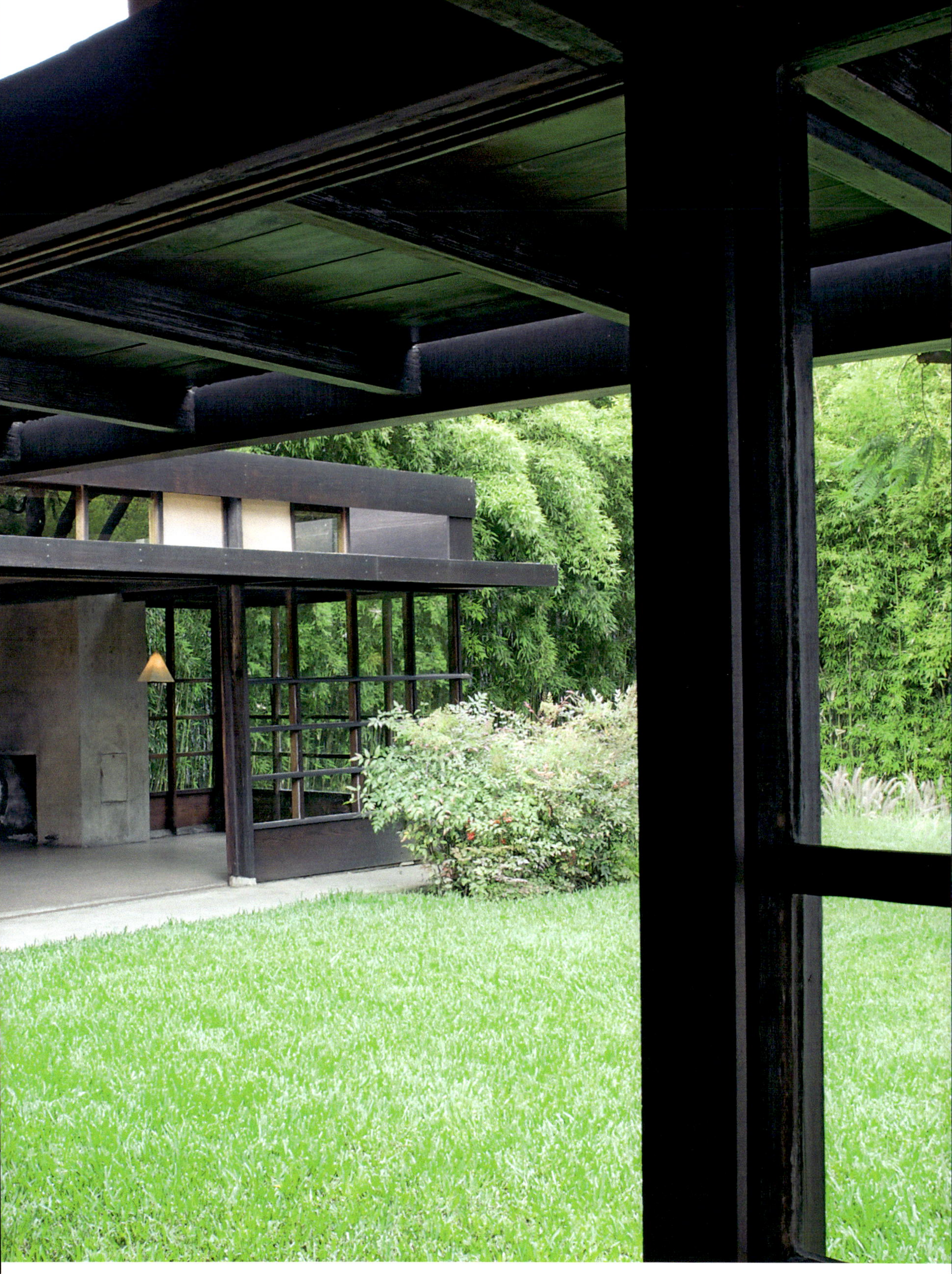

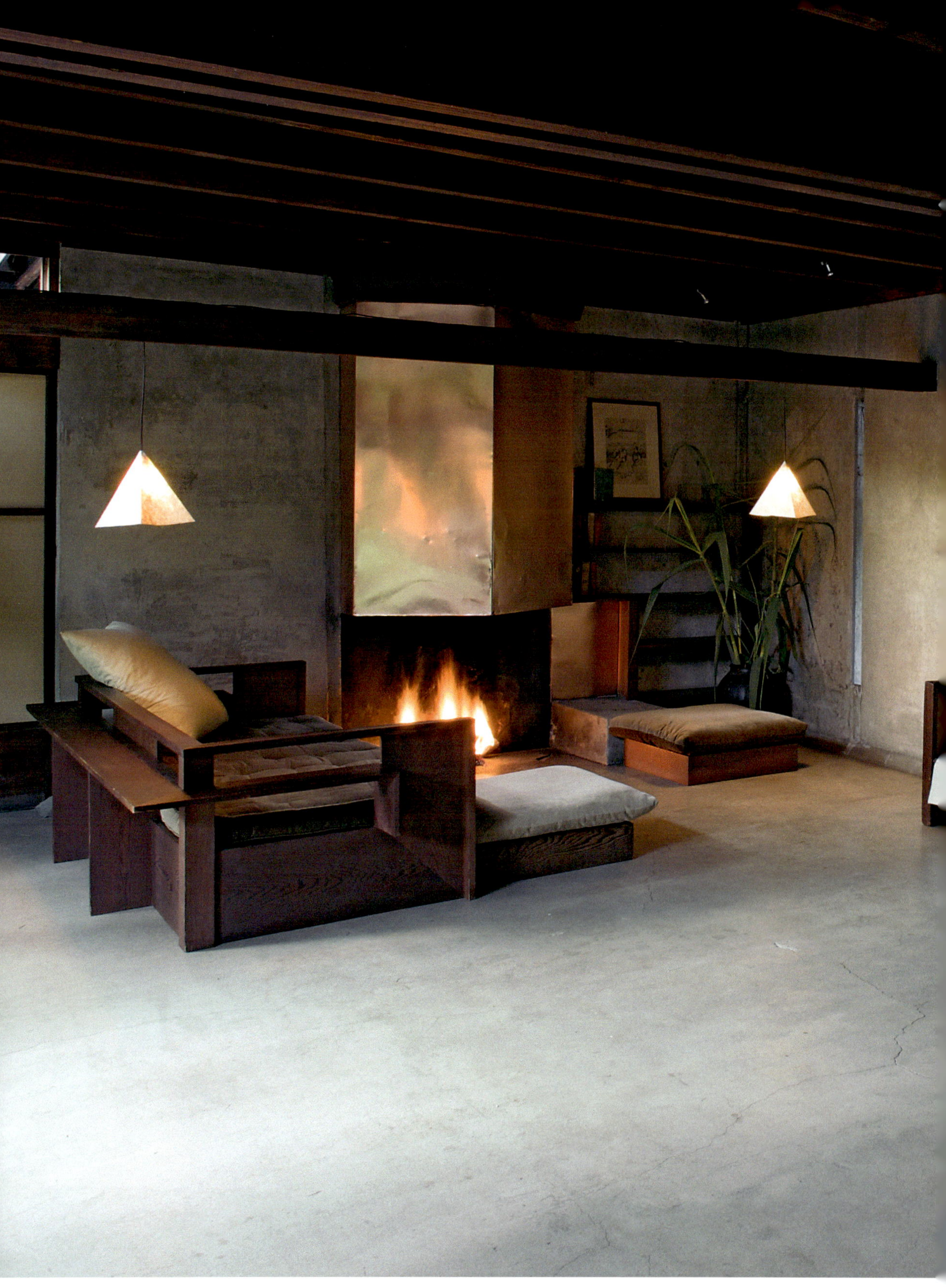

PLATE 30 S. P. G. studio, with original and reproduction furniture arranged according to a photograph taken in the 1920s by Roger Sturtevant.

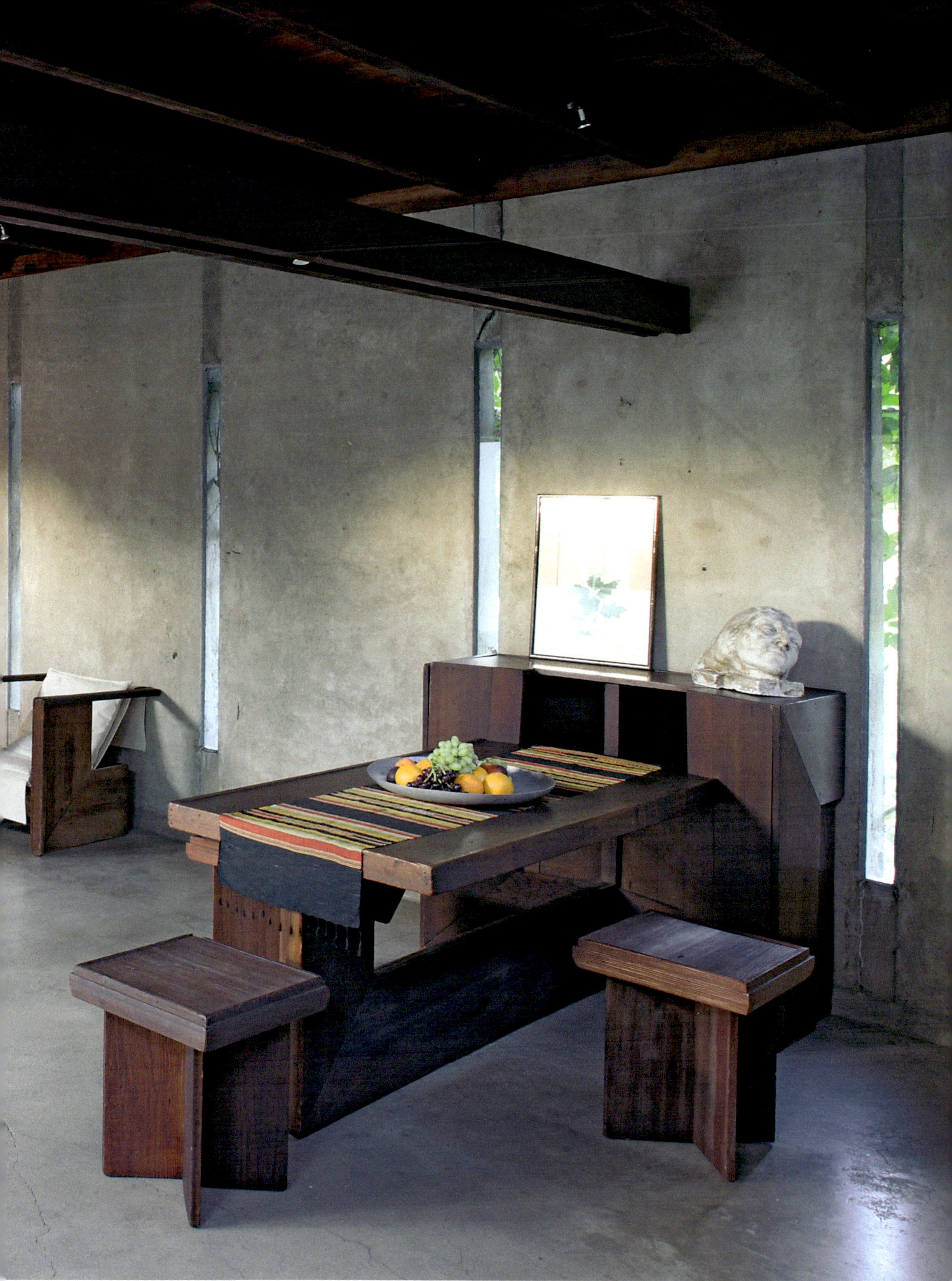

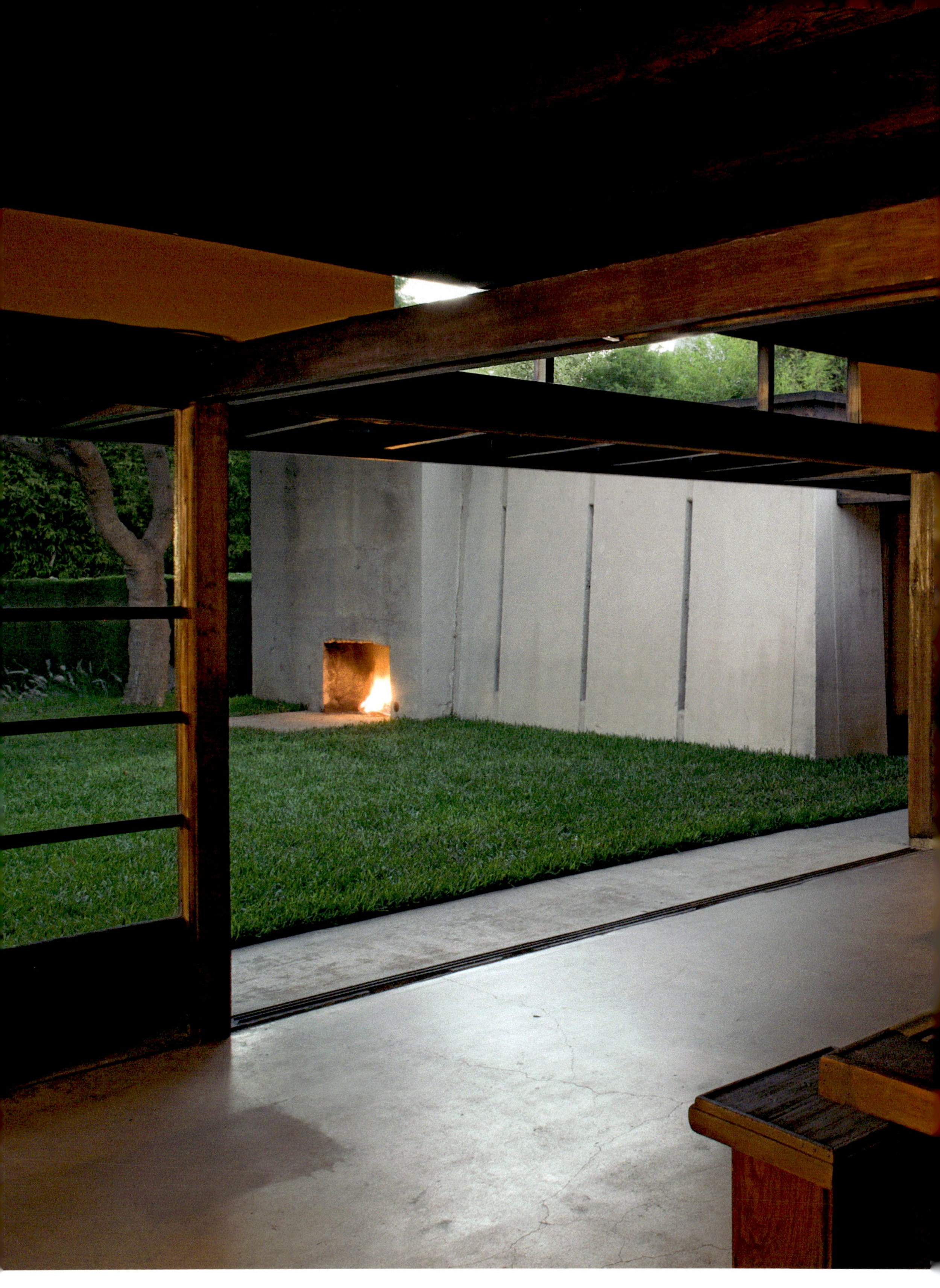

PLATE 31 S. P. G. studio, looking into the Schindler patio.

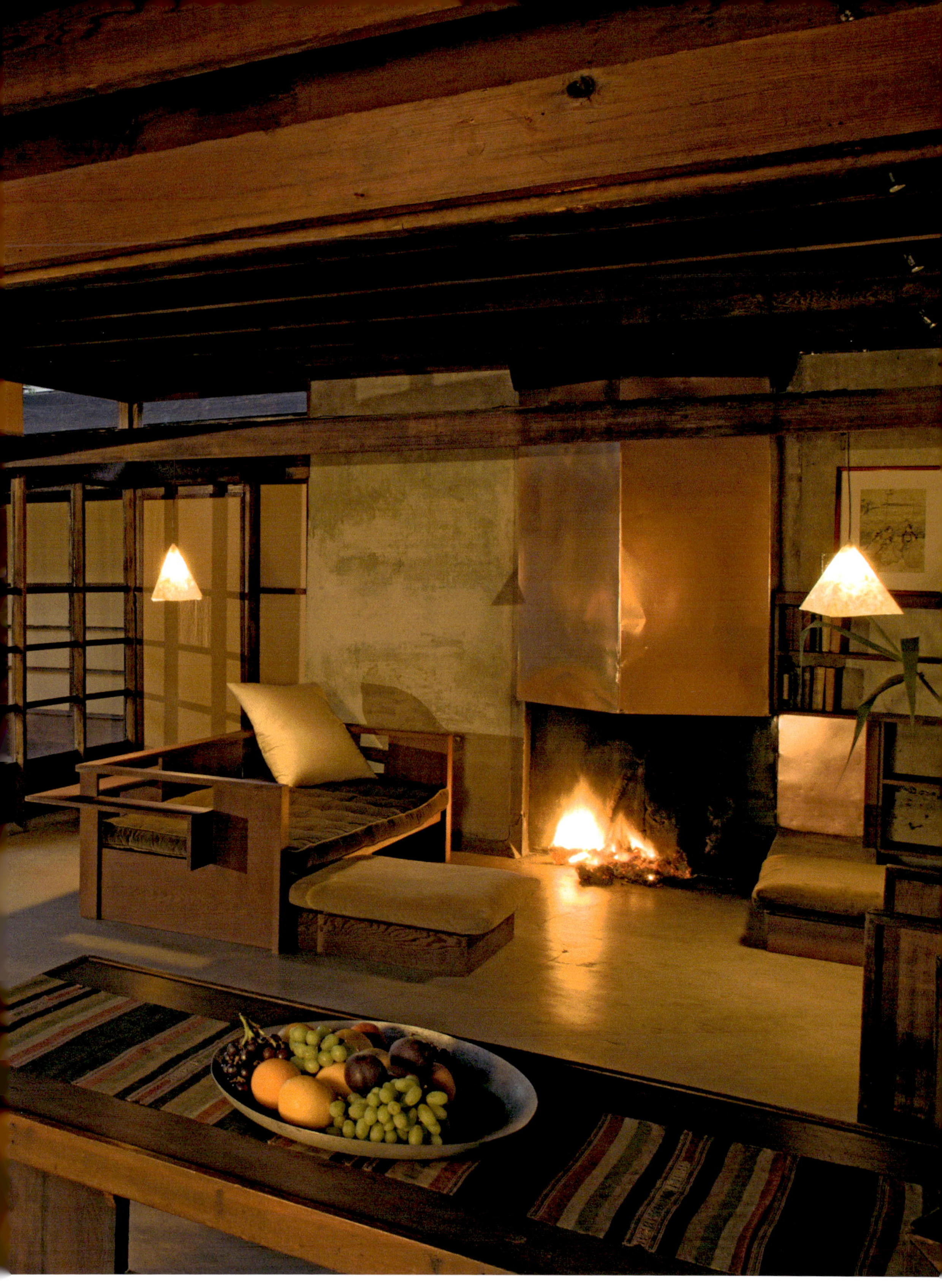

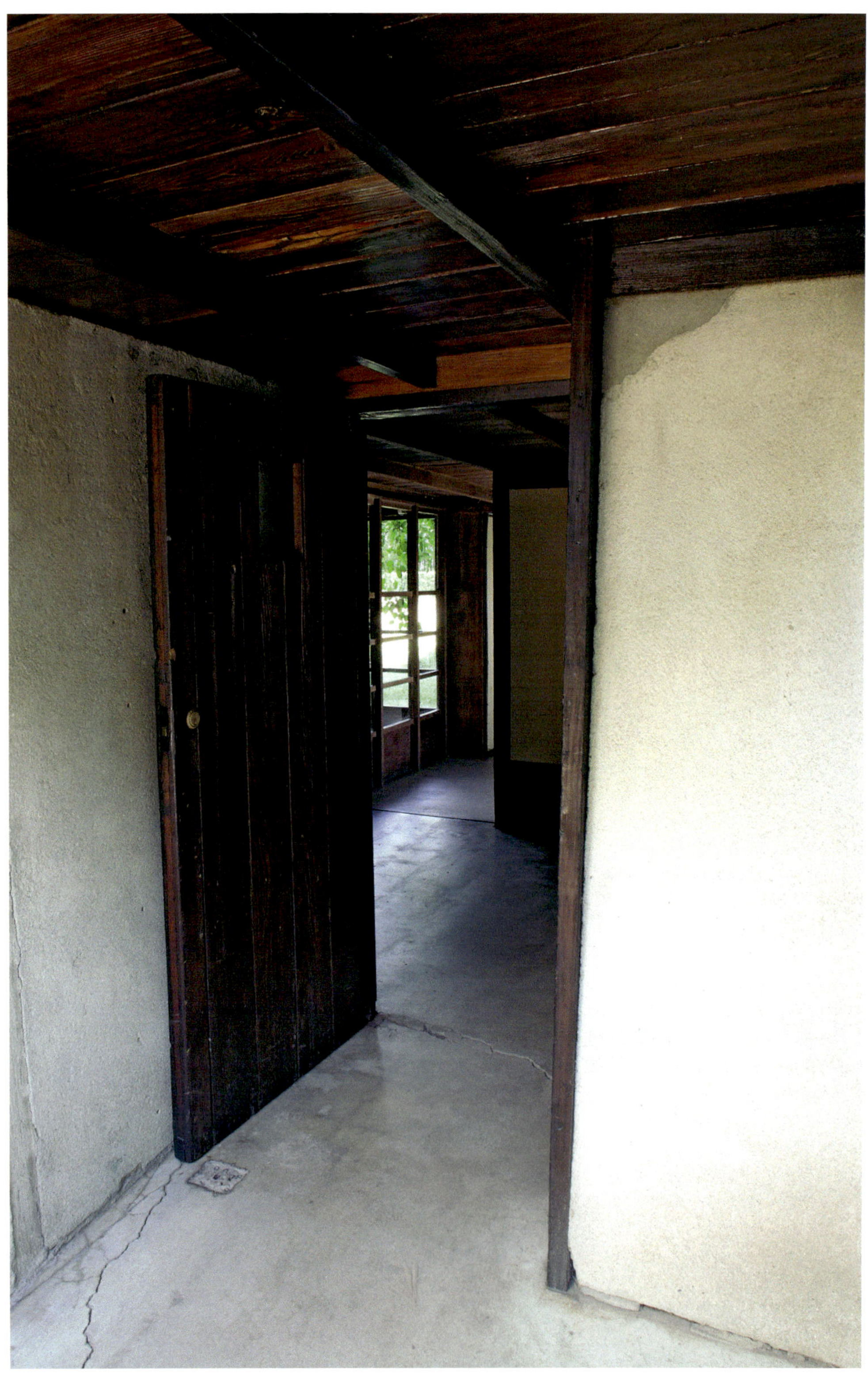

PLATE 32 Chace entry.

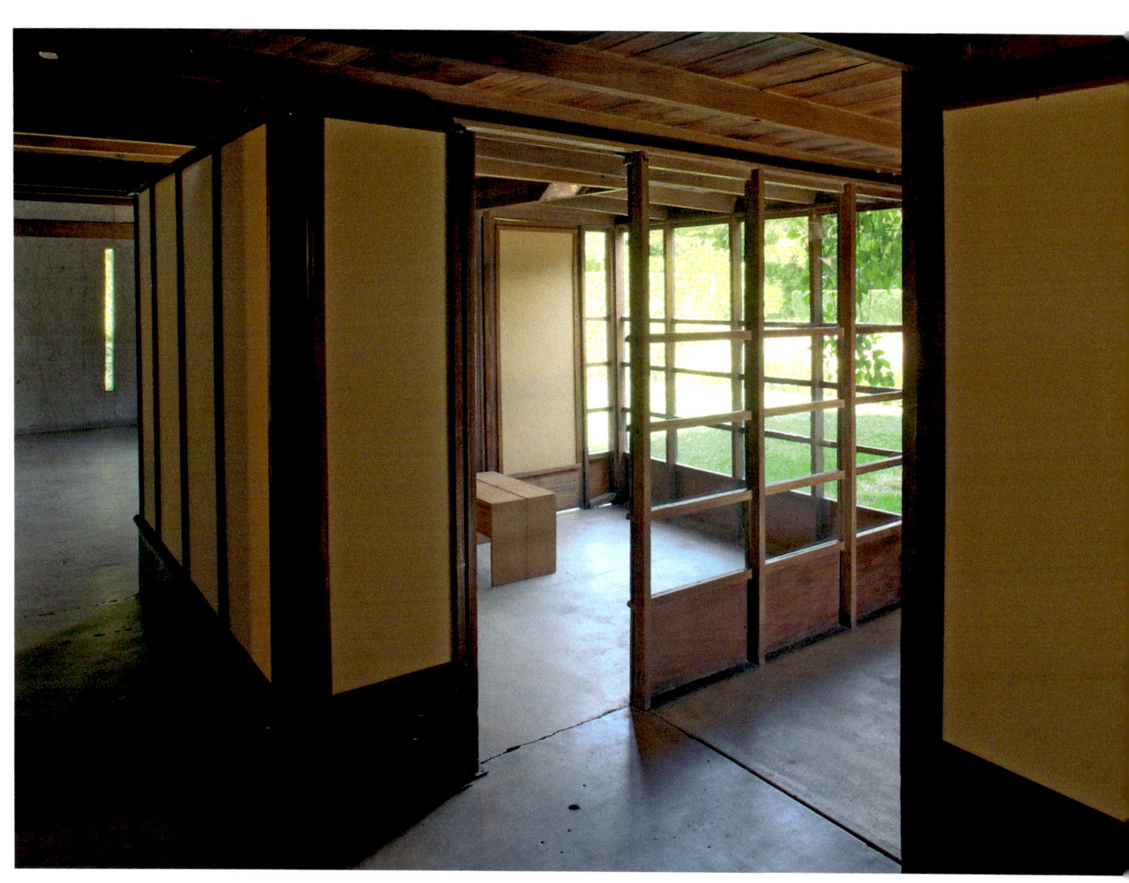

PLATE 33 Chace entry looking into the nursery.

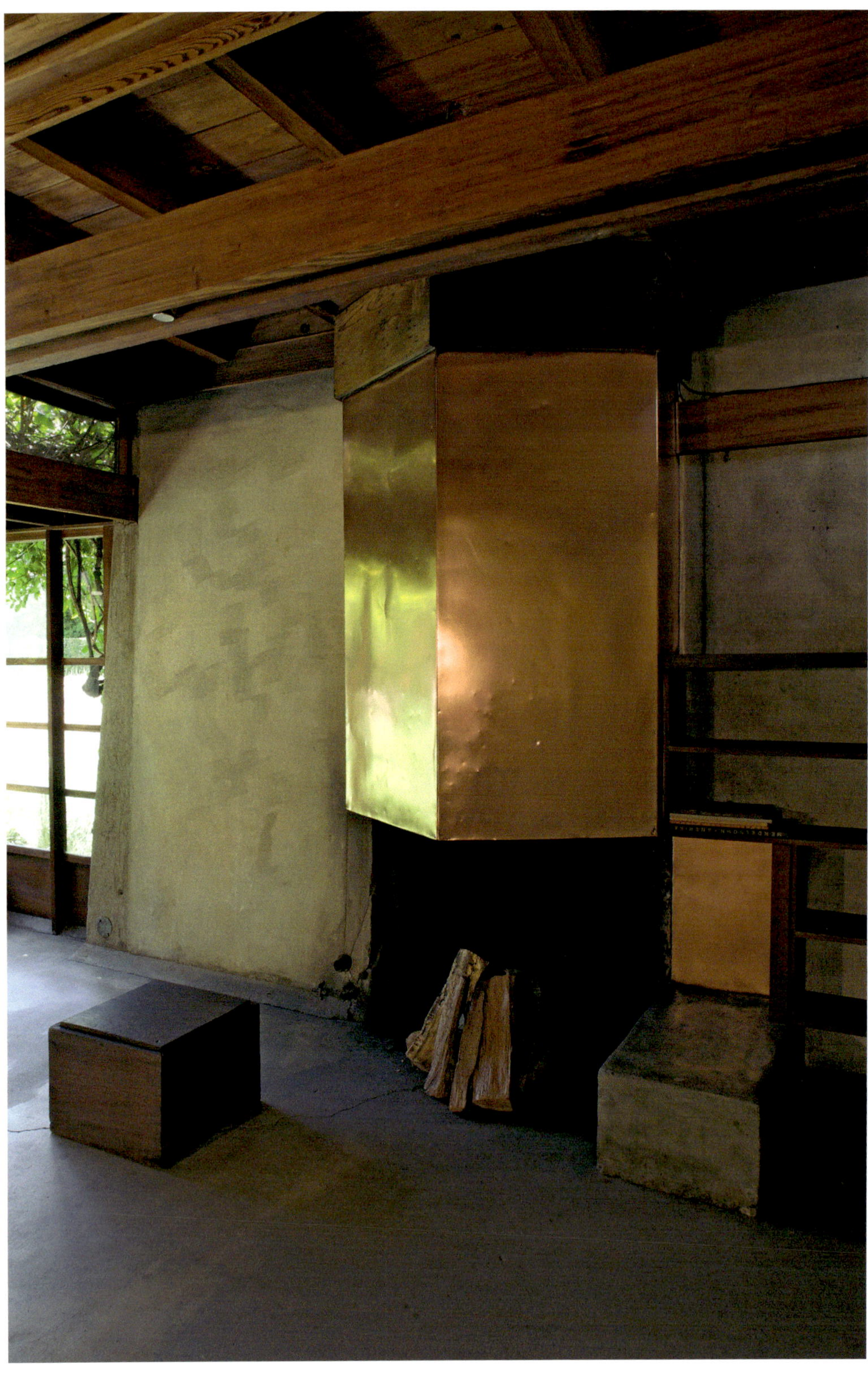

PLATE 34 M.D.C. studio.

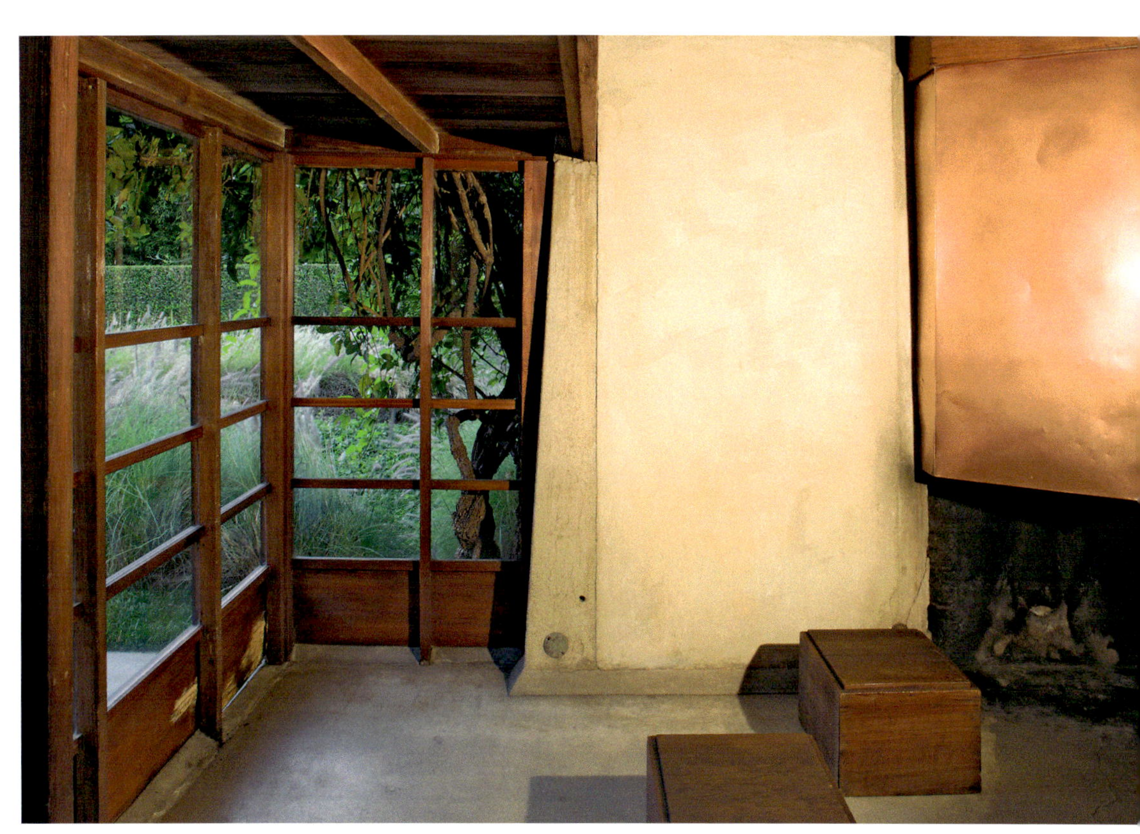

PLATE 35 M.D.C. studio.

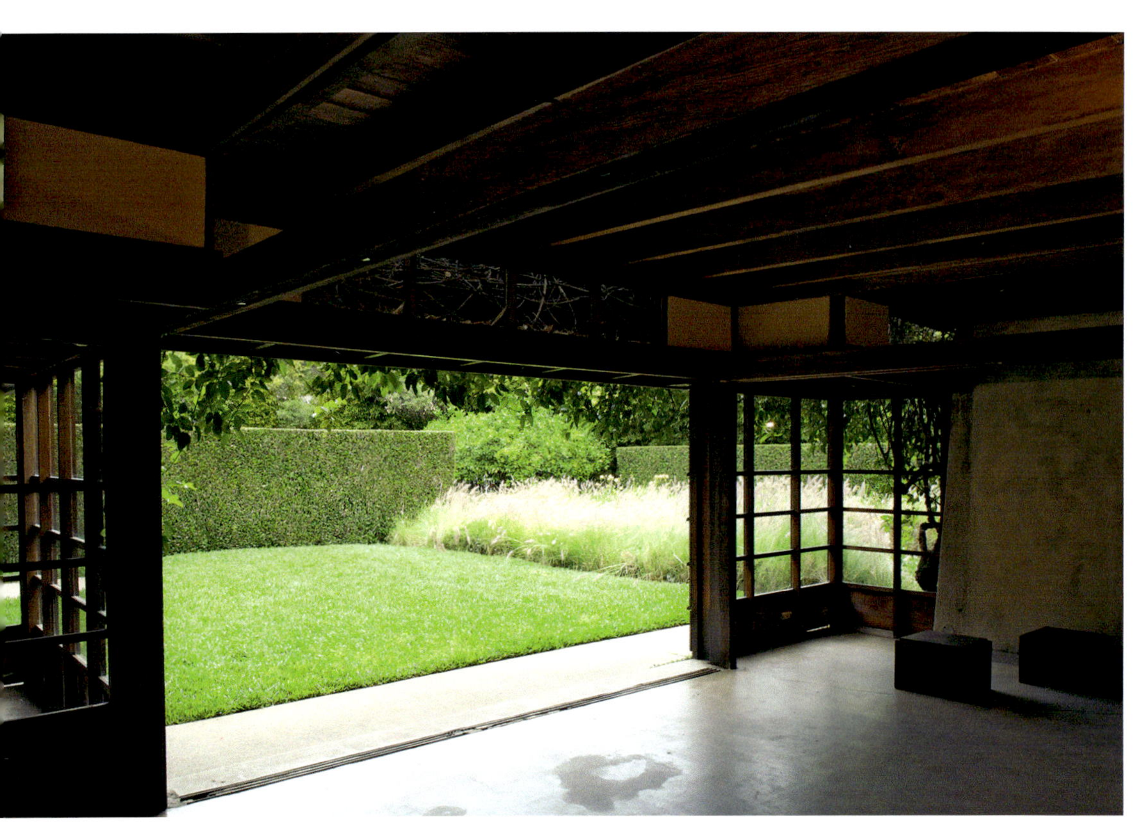

PLATE 36 M.D.C. studio, looking southeast into the Chace patio.

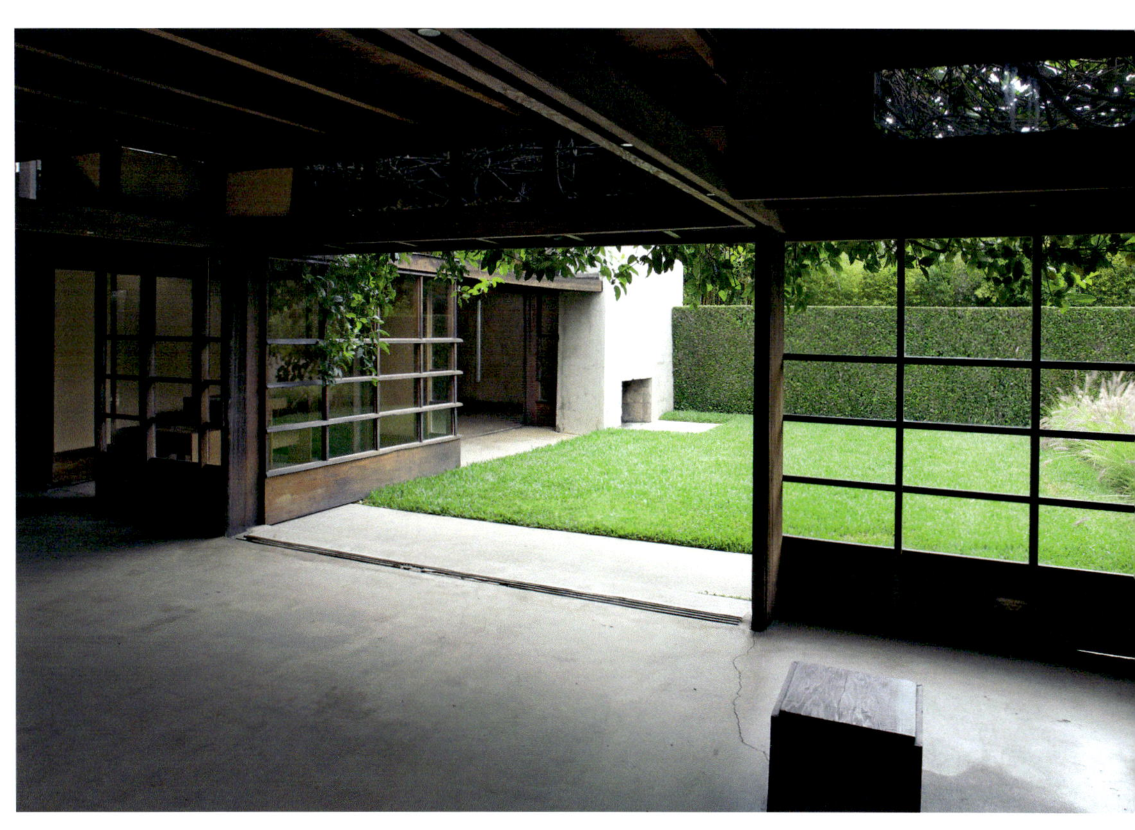

PLATE 37 M. D. C. studio, looking into the Chace patio.

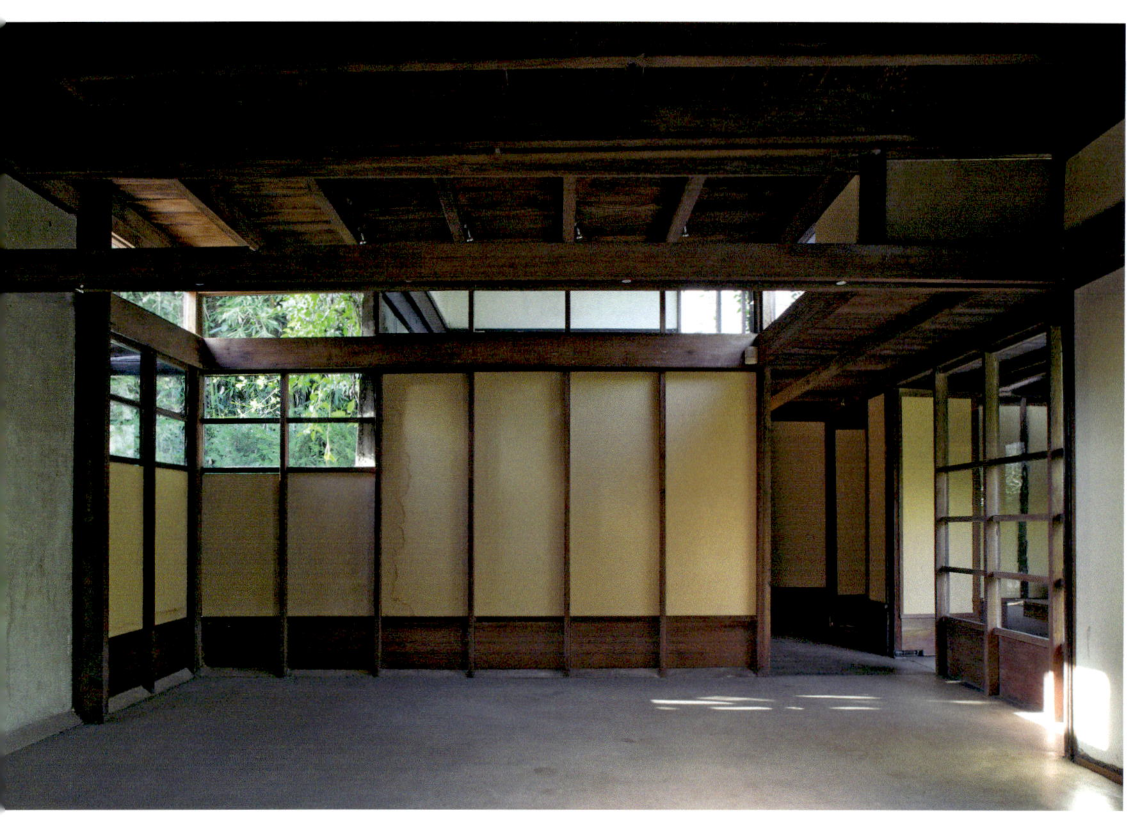

PLATE 38 M. D. C. studio, looking north.

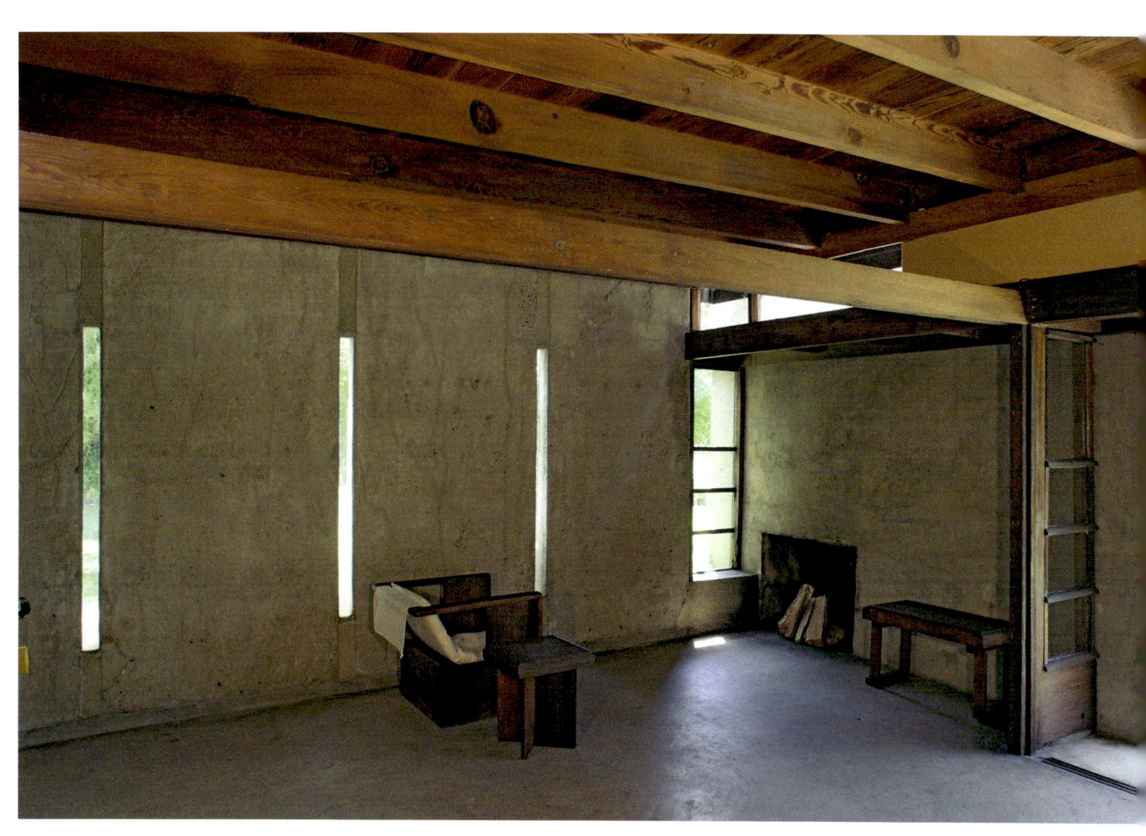

PLATE 39 C. B. C. studio.

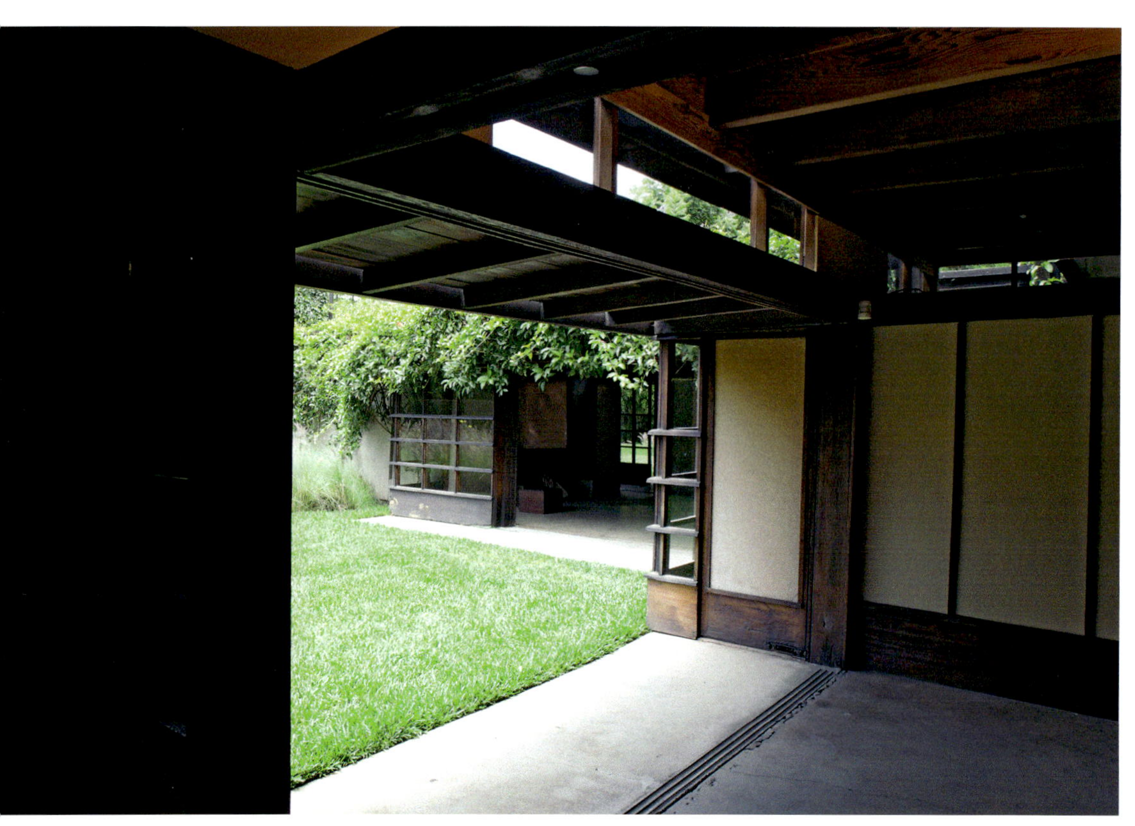

PLATE 40 C. B. C. studio, looking into the Chace patio.

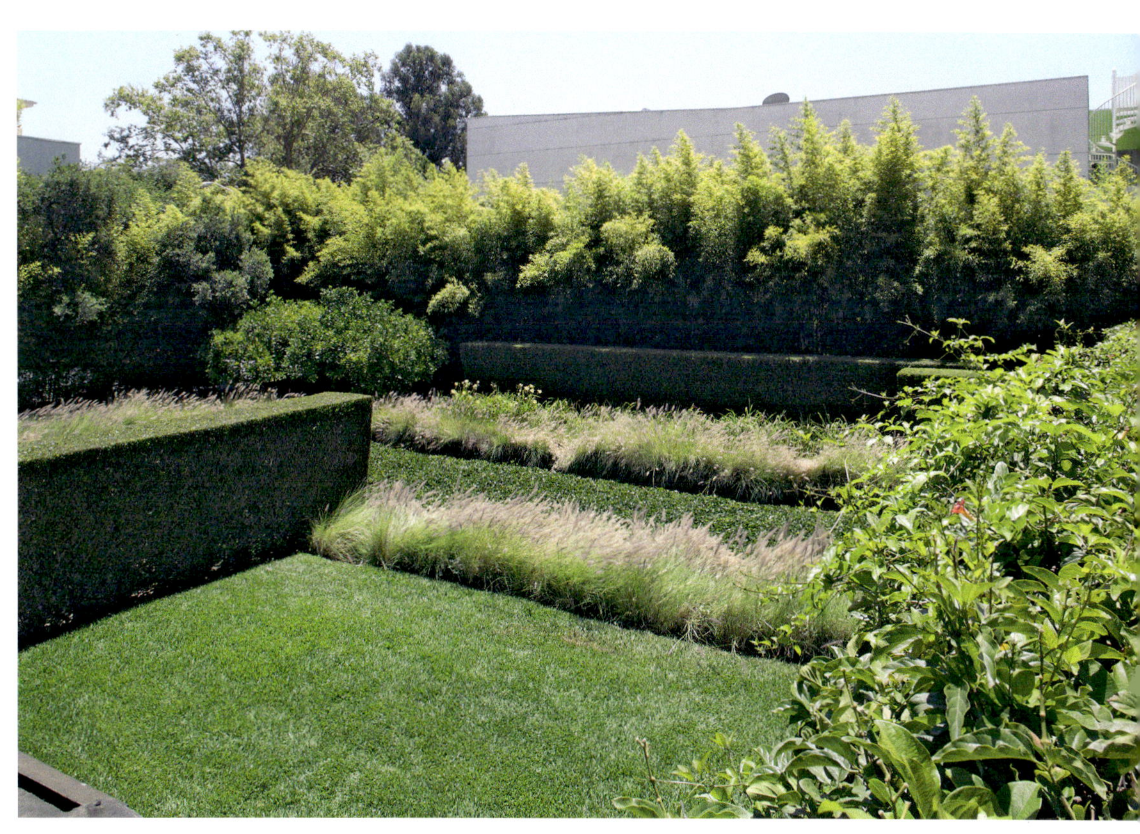

PLATE 41 Chace patio and the front garden, looking southeast.

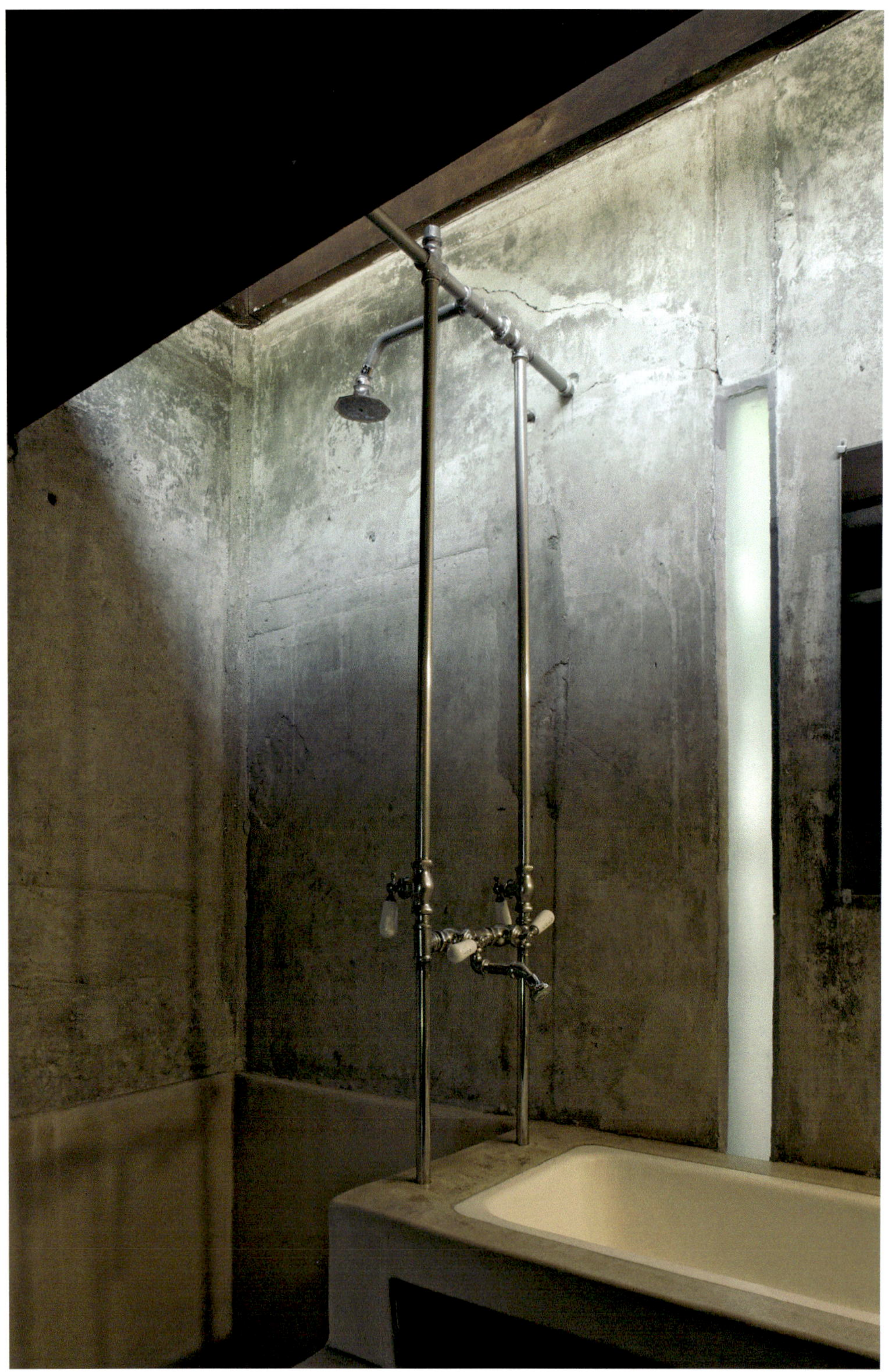

PLATE 42 Schindler bath.

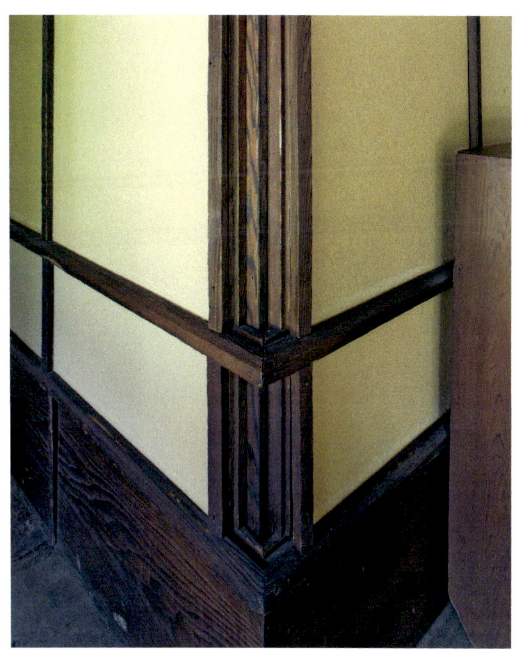

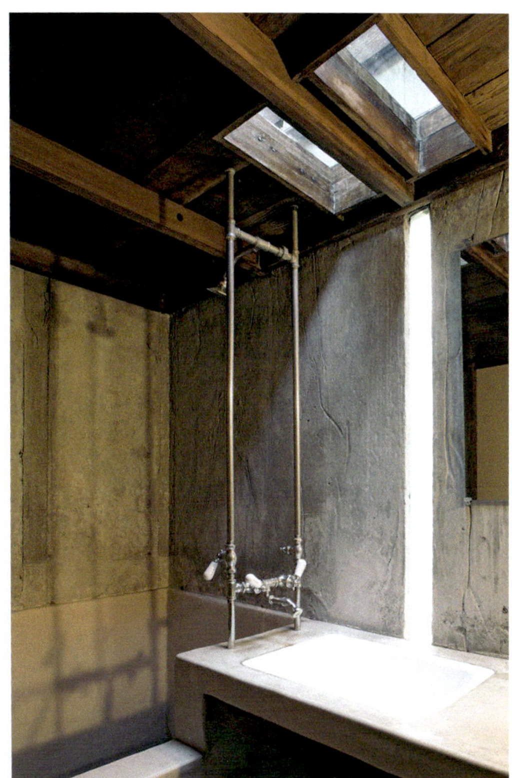

PLATE 43 R. M. S. studio, corner detail.

PLATE 44 Chace bath.

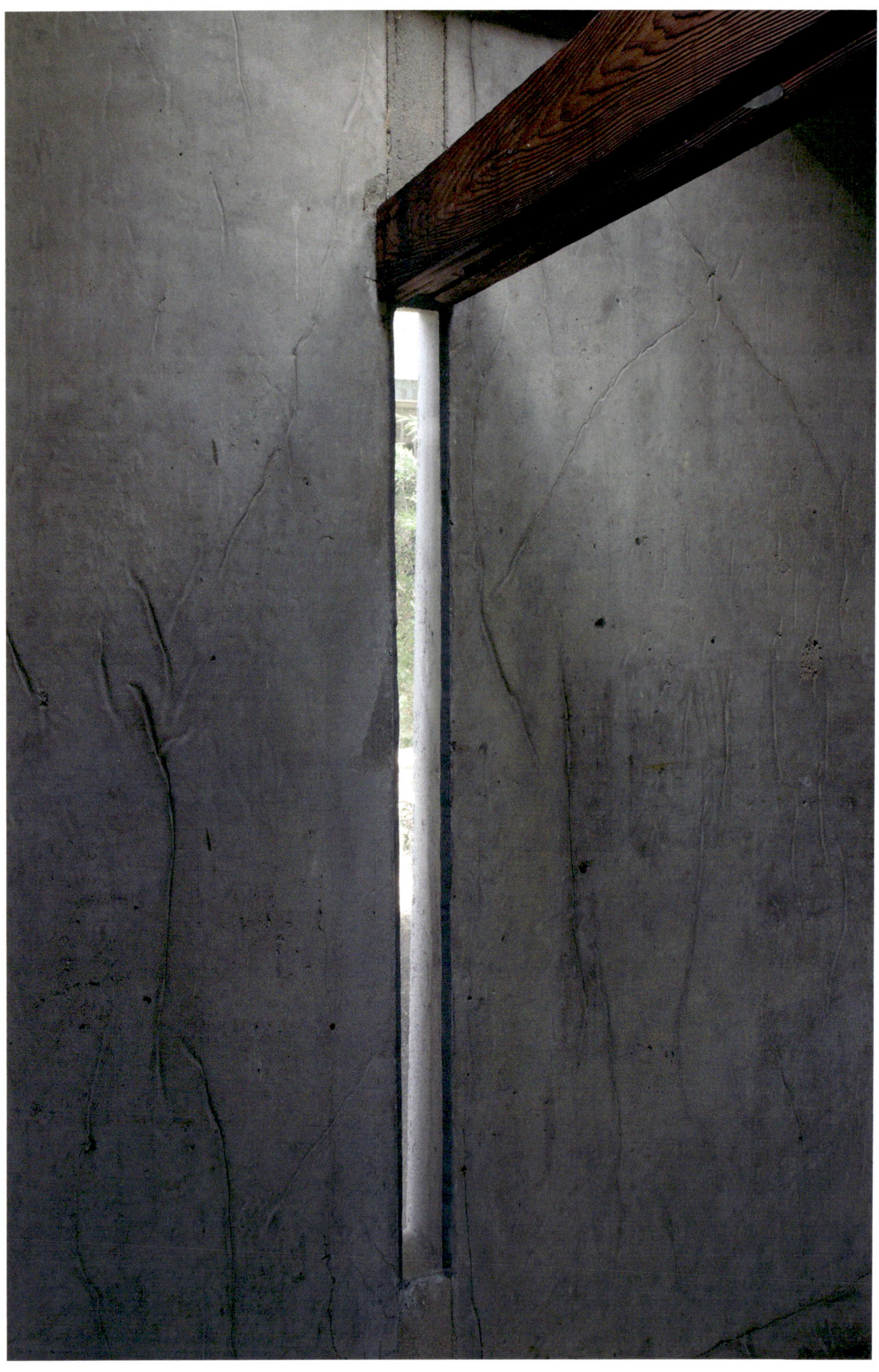

PLATE 45 C. B. C. studio, north wall.

THE KINGS ROAD HOUSE
PRE-EVERYBODY[1]

JUDITH SHEINE

For he was one of the originals of our time, and it's all there from the very first house he built as an independent designer.
REYNER BANHAM, 1975[2]

R. M. SCHINDLER'S HOUSE on Kings Road was so startlingly original that when it was finished in 1922, no one besides Schindler really knew what to make of it. The house resembled none that had come before. It lacked conventional rooms, such as living rooms or bedrooms; an obvious front; or any distinction between its materials of construction and its finish materials; and it made little distinction between the inside and the outside. Schindler was quite certain that the house was a great breakthrough. He wrote to his friend from Vienna, Richard Neutra, who was working for Erich Mendelsohn in Berlin, "My house is an interesting experiment and a success."[3] But he may have been the only one convinced of this at the time.

Like much of Schindler's work, the house was not widely recognized for its originality and significance until after the architect's death, and at the time it was built, it mystified even most architects. In the summer of 1922, Schindler sent a plan of the house to Louis Sullivan, who wrote to him, "Some weeks since I rec'd from you a blue print purporting to be the plan of a dwelling. But as no letter came with it I was unable to make it out."[4] The specific form of the house may have been new, but Schindler had been working out the ideas and principles behind its design since his time as a student in Vienna. There, during his studies with Otto Wagner and Adolf Loos, he learned to integrate theory and practice, which he continued to do throughout his career, writing and lecturing as well as designing and building. Wagner's ideas about the aesthetic possibilities of new materials and methods of construction, and Loos's rejection of architectural ornament and his emphasis on three-dimensional space, expressed in his sectionally complex interiors, as well as his interest in America and American technology, all strongly influenced Schindler.[5] However, Frank Lloyd Wright's influence may have been the strongest, leading Schindler to rethink even the radical architectural ideas he encountered in Vienna.

About 1912, Schindler wrote a manifesto he called "Modern Architecture: A Program."[6] Although this text was clearly influenced by a number of architect-theorists, even this early in his career his ideas had developed beyond those of any of his masters.[7] While Wagner believed that new building technologies would lead to new architectural forms, Schindler made the radical assertion, "The twentieth century is the first to abandon construction as a source for architectural form." Instead of having to build by sculpting a structural mass material, the architect was now freed by technological advances in the use of steel and reinforced concrete to design architecture using "the new medium of his art: SPACE." This notion of the primacy of space is linked to both Loos and Wright, with common origins in the work of Gottfried Semper. Schindler found Semper's idea of the "primitive hut," as a skeletal construction covered in hides, to be similar to modern skeletal construction with a variety of infill materials, and he concluded that the specific materials of construction were unimportant; what mattered was what these materials enclosed or defined: space.[8] Schindler took the definition of architecture as abstract space further than Semper or Loos in abandoning a requirement for any particular form of enclosure or for the house to serve as protection against the elements or the outside world. Inspired by Wright's work and his introductory essay in *Ausgeführte Bauten und Entwürfe von Frank Lloyd Wright,* known as the Wasmuth portfolio, published in 1911, Schindler embraced Wright's idea that technological advances (in heating and plumbing) made it possible for buildings to be integrated into their environments rather than act as a protection from them.[9] In his manifesto Schindler went one step further than Wright, integrating the outside environment into the modern dwelling by calling for the architect's "complete control of: space, climate, light, mood." Schindler proposed a radical reintegration of interior and exterior space in what he came to call his Space Architecture, the first fully realized example of which was his own house on Kings Road.

Although Schindler had rejected construction as the source for architectural form, the house displayed its constructive materials, both inside and out, more directly than any of Wagner's designs. The house was free of ornament, and the section was manipulated to define space not only inside but in the exterior patios as well, extending Loos's ideas outside. Schindler took Wright's principles of integration with the site, horizontality, dynamic and asymmetrical planning, and his flat roofs and clerestory windows and extended them all much further than Wright had, to that date, imagined; in the Kings Road house interior and exterior spaces are, essentially, continuous, connecting through the glass walls and sliding canvas doors, with the floors at the same level as the patios.

The Kings Road house absorbs and transforms ideas and principles from a large number of sources, including vernacular ones. The influence of Japanese designs that Schindler had seen in prints at Taliesin and Wright's Oak Park studio could be seen in the house's lightweight translucent sliding doors and geometric discipline, which, however, emphasized the connections to the outside spaces more than those between interior rooms.[10] The massive adobe walls he saw on his 1915 trip to New Mexico were translated into separate concrete slabs tapering in profile from bottom to top, with slots of glass between them, rendering the heavy walls almost screenlike. The patios of the missions and adobe houses of Southern California had been absorbed into architect Irving Gill's work, with which Schindler was familiar, having seen it initially on his 1915 trip to Los Angeles and San Diego and later when he moved to Southern California. Gill's Dodge House (1914–16) was only a block away on Kings Road, and Clyde Chace's experience with Gill, who had used a different form of tilt-slab construction in his La Jolla Woman's Club (1913–14), was helpful in developing the specific form of tilt-slab concrete construction used in the Kings Road house. However, the site plan, in which the house turned its back to the street and was completely open to the patios through glazing and sliding canvas doors, was clearly different from both Gill's work and the Spanish-inspired haciendas.[11] The site plan does, however, have another American precedent: From his time in Chicago, Schindler must have been familiar with H. H. Richardson's Glessner House (1885–87). Its site plan is an L shape that edges right up to the street, its heavy wall punctuated with slit windows, while large windows open to the private interior court. However, while all of these sources can be read in the Kings Road house, Schindler synthesized them into something that was truly original.

Much of what Schindler introduced in the Kings Road house set the pattern for his future work in Southern California: a site plan balancing interior and exterior spaces, in that the house could be read as a figure in the landscape or the figures of the patios and gardens could be read against the background of the house; the house closed to the street and open to private patios defined by an L-shaped structure; interior continuity with exterior spaces; diagonal, asymmetric planning; and sectional manipulation to create spatial hierarchies and to allow light to enter interior spaces from unexpected directions. A number of these features also set a precedent for the work of many other architects, including Wright, Neutra, Gregory Ain, Harwell Hamilton Harris, and Raphael Soriano. All of these architects would have been familiar with the house through visiting it in person (Wright), working there (Harris and Ain worked for Neutra at Kings Road, and both Ain and Soriano worked briefly for Schindler), or, in the case of Neutra, by living there.

It is also entirely possible that the Kings Road house both preceded and directly influenced developments in Europe. Both Kathryn Smith and Lionel March have made arguments leading to this conclusion. In her 2001 book *R. M. Schindler House* Smith makes the case that the Kings Road house was the first Modern house built in Europe or America, as it predated Walter Gropius's Experimental House (1922–23), Le Corbusier's House at Vaucresson and Ozenfant Studio (both 1923), and Gerrit Rietveld's Schröder House (1924). Earlier, Smith had established that the Kings Road house footprint, the three L-shaped wings rotating clockwise in a pinwheel pattern, had preceded the use of a similar plan by Mies van der Rohe in his 1923 Concrete Country House and by Gropius in the 1925–26 Bauhaus at Dessau.[12] Lionel March took this argument one step further, suggesting that the plans for the house may have been in Berlin in 1922.[13] Schindler and Neutra had maintained a correspondence starting when Schindler left Vienna for the United States. Neutra was working for Erich Mendelsohn in Berlin in 1922, and the two architects discussed their respective architectural work and the possibility of Neutra coming to America. In a June 16, 1922, letter to Neutra, Schindler described the house and its concrete construction; at the end of the letter is a postscript in which Schindler asked, "Did you receive [word illegible]?"[14] March speculated that the illegible word was *blueprint,* and that if Neutra had received the blueprint, he could have shown it to Mendelsohn and Mies. It is likely that Schindler sent a blueprint to Neutra; he had sent one to his father-in-law in Chicago; to Will Smith, a draftsman working at Taliesin; and, as noted previously, to Sullivan. If, in fact, that was the case, then it is entirely possible that the Kings Road house not only preceded but also directly influenced subsequent European developments in modern architecture.

Schindler himself was convinced that his house was a precedent for both European and American Modern houses and made the case several times. Its radical form may have contributed to its not being published until ten years after it was built, although other concrete houses Schindler designed in the 1920s were published in the architectural press between 1927 and 1930, including Pueblo Ribera Court (1923), the How House (1925), and the Lovell Beach House (1922–26).[15] The Kings Road house was published in February 1932 after Maxwell Levinson, the editor of *T-Square,* asked Schindler to submit material of his choice for publication. Schindler sent photos and a description of the Kings Road house:

> Although the house was built ten years ago, it is of special interest just now. It initiates a development in residence building, which was recently furthered by Mies van der Rohe in his model residence at the German [*sic:* Berlin] Building Exposition [fig. 24]. Although my house is speaking in different materials a different language, it says essentially the same thing.[16]

That issue of *T-Square* also included articles by Wright, Le Corbusier, and Buckminster Fuller.[17]

Wright had visited the Kings Road house in 1922 and 1923, but it is likely that he saw it again in *T-Square* in 1932, at a time when he was looking to reinvent his architecture. Schindler and Wright had a complex relationship. Schindler saw Wright as the first space architect; he described the work he had first seen illustrated in the Wasmuth portfolio and later in person in America as being free from tradition. He wrote, "The room is not a box—the walls have disappeared—and Nature flows in total freedom through the houses—keeping the roof as a wide, necessary shelter."[18] However, Schindler was disappointed by what he saw as a return to an older, sculptural form of architecture in Wright's work in Los Angeles in the 1920s, houses carved out of mass structural materials with references to traditional Mayan architecture.[19] Nevertheless, Schindler continued to admire Wright, particularly his early work, even while moving beyond him in the Kings Road house. Although Wright would certainly not acknowledge it, the influence does not seem to have been only one-way; while the Kings Road house borrowed from Wright's houses, Wright

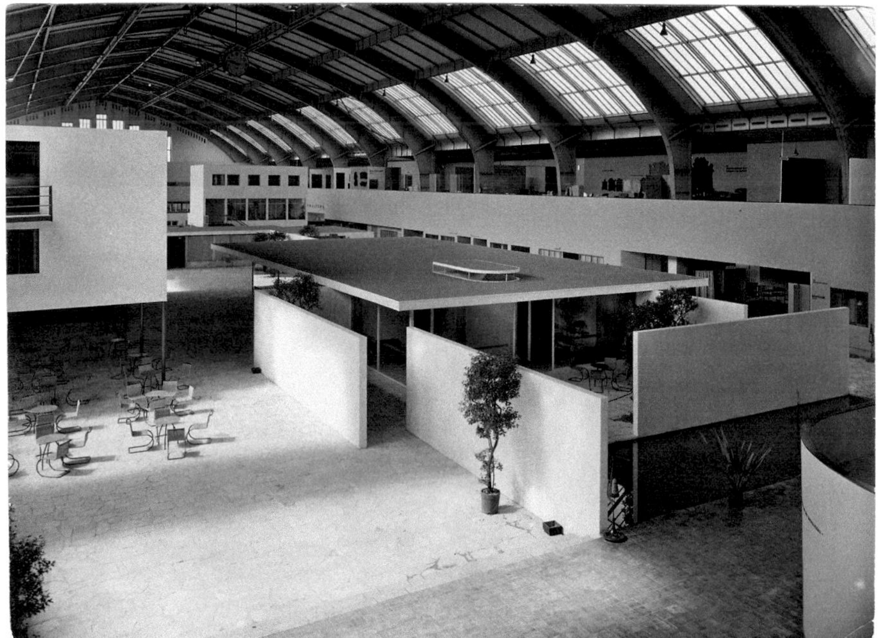

24 Ludwig Mies van der Rohe (1886–1969), 1931 Berlin Building Exposition model house. Mies van der Rohe, Ludwig (1886–1969) © ARS, NY. Deutsche Bauausstellung Berlin, Germany, view of the exposition, 1931. Silver-gelatin print, 6 ⅝ × 9 ⅛" (16.8 × 23.2 cm). Mies van der Rohe Archive, gift of the architect. (MMA1135) The Museum of Modern Art, New York, NY, U.S.A. Digital Image © The Museum of Modern Art/Licensed by SCALA/Art Resource, NY.

seems to have borrowed even more directly from Kings Road for his Usonian houses. The first of these simple, relatively inexpensive, flat-roofed, one-story houses was designed in 1933.[20] Both the Kings Road house and a number of the Usonian houses had L-shaped plans with plumbing at the knuckle; nearly solid walls facing the outside world; glass walls and doors connecting to the private, outdoor space at the rear; and a systematized method of construction. The first of the built Usonian houses, the Herbert Jacobs House (1936; fig. 25), demonstrates all of these features, which likely work less well with the climate in Wisconsin.

But Wright was not the only architect to deploy these features; as Schindler noted in 1932, Ludwig Mies van der Rohe and others had also used them, even if the direct influence was not as evident. Schindler attempted to set the record straight a number of times regarding the precedence of his house. In 1947, *Architectural Forum* published a letter Schindler wrote to the editors, suggesting some revisions to the dates and examples used in the outline of contemporary architecture that had appeared in the May issue. Schindler noted that his Lovell Beach House of 1926 had predated developments in 1929 that had been illustrated by Neutra's Lovell Health House and Le Corbusier's Villa Savoye. He went

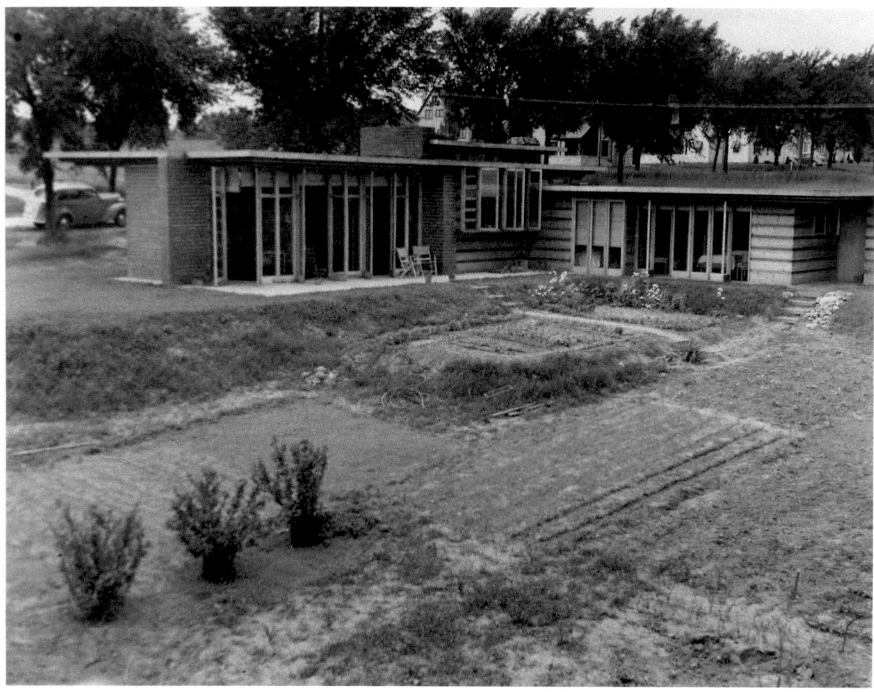

25 Frank Lloyd Wright, Herbert Jacobs House, Madison, Wisconsin, 1936. Photograph © Susan Jacobs Lockhart.

on to point out that he had built his own house in 1922, which had

> become the prototype for most of the now fashionable California houses. It introduced the following characteristic features:
>
> A cellarless, rambling, one-story building, low on the ground, the floor extending without step into the garden.
>
> A full-height glass wall with large sliding doors on the patio side, under ample overhangs.
>
> A flat shed roof with clerestory windows.
>
> A solid back wall for privacy, and movable partitions for flexibility.
>
> The wall construction uses a prefabricated standard concrete wall unit.[21]

The Kings Road house was clearly a direct precedent for the work of many modern architects practicing in California. Neutra's work, beginning in the late 1930s, began to exhibit some of these features in, for example, the Garden House (1939) that he built behind his own VDL Research House of 1932, and, perhaps even more directly, in the Kaufmann House in Palm Springs and the Bailey House (both 1946). The latter was Neutra's only built design for the well-known Case Study House program sponsored by John Entenza and published in his magazine *Arts and Architecture* from 1945 to 1962. The Case Study houses and many designed outside the program—largely flat-roofed, closed to the street, and open through glazing to private patios—designed by Neutra, Soriano, Craig Ellwood, Pierre Koenig, and others, clearly make reference to the Kings Road house (for example, fig. 26). Schindler pointed this out in his response to a questionnaire about his work from the School of Architecture at the University of Southern California for its Directory of Contemporary Architecture, dated October 10, 1949:

> To illustrate my principles I built my own house. . . . It was the first house to break with Eastern tradition and to respond to the climate and living conditions of Southern California. It introduced such characteristic features of the present contemporary house as merging of outdoor and indoor space and living.

Although Schindler continued to campaign for the originality of the Kings Road house, it wasn't until after his death that the house began to receive attention as the truly unprecedented work that it was. Esther McCoy gave Schindler his first significant exposure when she included him in her 1960 work *Five California Architects.*[22] European visitors such as Reyner Banham, Hans Hollein, and Herman Hertzberger came to Los Angeles in the 1960s and began to write about the Schindler work they found, and David Gebhard produced the first monograph on the architect's work, *Schindler,* in 1971.[23]

However, despite being a precedent for much modern work, the house is not conventional Modern architecture and certainly not International Style—it's Space Architecture. For Schindler the primary consideration in design was the interior space, its articulation and connection to the exterior, rather than what a building was made out of or looked like. In his 1934 article "Space Architecture," Schindler repudiated the International Style and its dependence on the machine, dismissing its practitioners as mere functionalists along with the entire notion of "styles" in architecture.[24] Unfortunately for Schindler's career and reputation, the International Style proponents also repudiated him.

In 1932, the term *International Style* emerged from the first architecture exhibition held at the Museum of Modern Art in New York. Called "Modern Architecture—International Exhibition," it was curated by Henry-Russell Hitchcock and Philip Johnson, who also wrote the accompanying book, *The International Style: Architecture since 1922.*[25] The exhibit and book showcased the work of European and American practitioners including Mies van der Rohe, Le Corbusier, Gropius, and Neutra. While Wright was included in the exhibit, he was clearly presented as a figure from the past, with the others representing the future.[26] Despite the obviously Modern qualities of Schindler's Lovell Beach House, his work was not included in the show. Schindler had already had a fairly hostile exchange of letters with Hitchcock after the publication in 1929 of Hitchcock's *Modern Architecture: Romanticism and Reintegration,* in which Schindler attempted to correct Hitchcock's attribution of Wright's Imperial Hotel drawings to Neutra (Schindler had done them), and they had gotten into a nasty exchange about what was worth publishing and how best to publish it.[27] Schindler exchanged letters with Johnson about the exhibition in New York, with Johnson

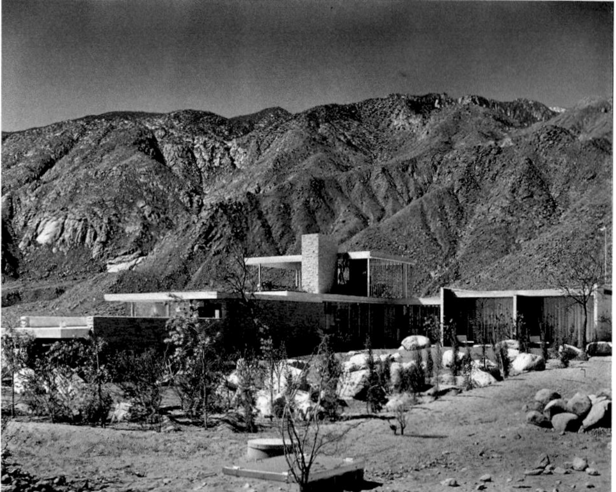

26 Richard J. Neutra, Kaufmann House, Palm Springs, California, 1946. © J. Paul Getty Trust. Used with permission. Julius Shulman Photography Archive, Research Library at the Getty Research Institute (2004.R.10).

telling him that there was no room for his work in that show but inviting him to send photos for the traveling show when it came to Los Angeles. Schindler had concluded by then that the exhibit was specifically about a certain style, the "so-called 'International Style,'" and that

> if this is the case, my work has no place in it. I am not a stylist, not a functionalist, nor any other sloganist. Each of my buildings deals with a different *architectural* problem, the existence of which has been entirely forgotten in this period of rational mechanization. The question of whether a house is really a house is more important to me, than the fact that it is made of steel, glass, putty, or hot air.[28]

In fact, Schindler was pointing out the differences between his Space Architecture and that of the International Stylists, reiterating the points that he had made in his manifesto two decades earlier. For Schindler, new materials and methods of construction did not define new architectural vocabulary; the space architect worked with "space, climate, light, mood" to design architecture. It's not clear that Hitchcock and Johnson understood this crucial distinction; needless to say, Schindler's work was not included in the Los Angeles exhibit, nor was it included in many significant future exhibits and publications of Modern architecture.

This kind of rejection limited the scale of commissions Schindler would receive; but although he was clearly bitter about his lack of recognition, it did not prevent him from pursuing his career in Los Angeles until his death in 1953. He somehow managed to stay busy, even during the Depression, building mostly single-family houses, half a dozen apartment buildings, a few commercial buildings, and one church. He designed over 500 projects, of which more than 150 were built—though some were tiny (small residential additions and remodels).

Schindler managed not only to continue to work, but also to develop his own original and inventive Space Architecture. In fact, one of the reasons he felt the need to repeatedly point out the achievements of his 1922 house is that he thought that contemporary practitioners continued to reproduce many of the features of the house while his own work had moved on. While Schindler's later work looked very different, the principles of his Space Architecture were almost all there in his first independent work. In, perhaps, a last attempt to convince the Museum of Modern Art of the special qualities of Space Architecture, Schindler reiterated this point in a 1952 letter to Arthur Drexler, sent in response to Drexler's request for material for an update to the museum's 1944 "Built in the USA" exhibit and catalog. Schindler sent photos of his Kallis (1946; fig. 27a, b) and Lechner (1948) houses and described two recently completed houses with translucent walls and roofs (probably the 1948–49 Janson and 1949–50 Tischler houses; fig. 28a, b), explaining that these houses represented a "final development" of the architecture he introduced in 1921–22:

> In my own house (1921) I introduced features which seemed to be necessary for life in California: an open plan, flat on the ground; living patios; glass walls; translucent walls; wide sliding doors; clerestory windows; shed roofs with wide shading overhangs. These features have now been accepted generally and form the basis of the contemporary California house.[29]

The letters and photos were not successful in convincing Drexler of the significance of his Space Architecture; Schindler's work was not included in the 1952 show. Schindler's complex late works were clearly too difficult for the eastern critics to understand.

Kings Road may have shared features with other Modern designs, but its specific spatial characteristics are what distinguished it and tied it to Schindler's later works rather than to Modern architects' designs that resembled Kings Road. Schindler's work changed in appearance over the years, sometimes radically. He was always looking for ways to build as inexpensively as possible, first for himself at Kings Road and later for his clients, who, especially during the Depression, tended to have more taste than money. Usually working as the contractor on his design projects, Schindler had more direct experience with construction systems and costs than most architects. While he valued the flexibility reinforced concrete allowed, as well as its ability to be used as both a structural and a finish material, he found that despite many experiments with methods attempting to build concrete economically (Slab-Tilt, Slab-Cast, sprayed-on concrete), by the 1930s he had to abandon it and build houses out of the less-expensive standard construction system, wood frame covered with stucco.[30] He developed his own vocabulary for this work, which he called Plaster Skin.[31] Never completely satisfied with his transformations of this construction system, he experimented with materials and forms and developed a variation of standard wood-frame construction that he introduced after World War II and called Schindler Frame. This system allowed him to expose more constructive materials, especially in the roofs, and he experimented with sloping roof forms and walls, as well as with new materials such as translucent fiberglass, producing effects that were often startling, at least to eastern critics. In his preface to David Gebhard's 1971 book, *Schindler,* Hitchcock quoted his own 1940 assessment of Schindler's work:

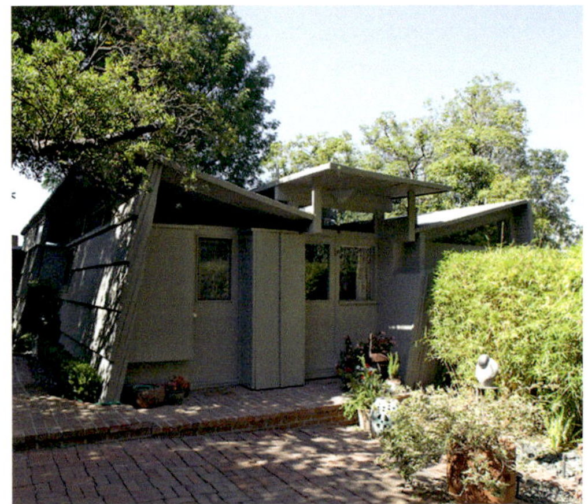

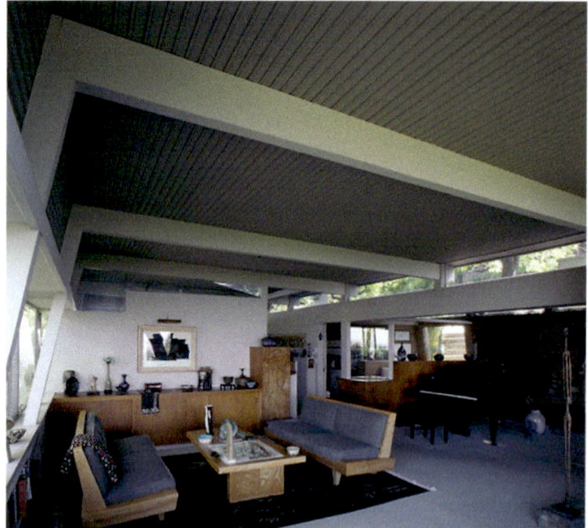

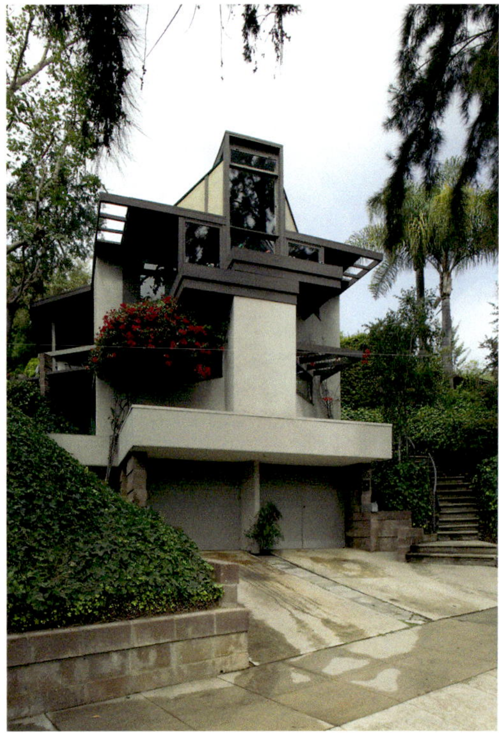

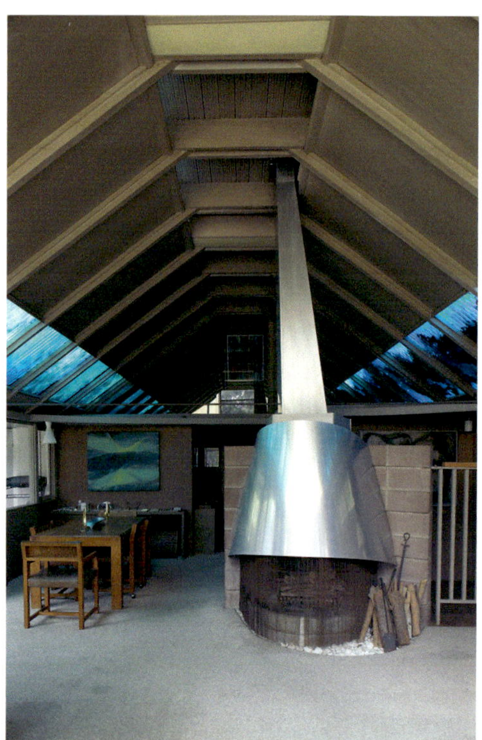

27A *(left above)* R.M. Schindler, Kallis House, 1946, Los Angeles, California: exterior view. © Timothy Sakamoto.

27B *(right above)* R.M. Schindler, Kallis House, Los Angeles, California: interior view. © Timothy Sakamoto.

28A *(left below)* R.M. Schindler, Tischler House, 1949–50, Los Angeles, California: exterior view. © Timothy Sakamoto.

28B *(right below)* R.M. Schindler, Tischler House, Los Angeles, California: interior view. © Timothy Sakamoto.

> The case of Schindler I do not profess to understand. There is certainly immense vitality, perhaps somewhat lacking among many of the best architects of the West Coast. But this vitality seems in general to lead to arbitrary and brutal effects.

Hitchcock did go on to say that he would certainly evaluate the work differently at present, acknowledging that for some of the directions Modern architecture had been moving post–World War II, "Schindler's work, already from the beginning of his productive career in the mid-twenties, was by its very variety premonitory."[32] However, one of the most interesting things about Schindler's work is that despite its great variety, it has significant spatial consistencies, most of which can be traced back to Kings Road.

Schindler's Space Architecture was primarily focused on the design of interior space and its connection to outside spaces and views. Each building was designed around the specifics of the site and the client.[33] Schindler sited houses to maximize usable outdoor space. When sites were too steeply sloped to develop a patio around which to place a house, he connected the interior to terraces, balconies, and views. As at the Kings Road house, his site plans achieved a balance between the figure of the house in the landscape and the figure of the outdoor space defined by the house. There was no residual space in Schindler site plans; houses were never objects sitting in a field, but, instead, completely integrated into their sites. As already noted, the houses were generally closed to the street and open to the private outdoor spaces. The simplest way to define such an outdoor space was with an L shape, and this is the plan type most commonly found in Schindler designs.[34]

This type of site planning led to plans that exhibited movement along diagonal axes. In Schindler plans, living spaces are generally entered from a corner, along a diagonal axis that extends through corner windows, which are ubiquitous in his work. While this type of planning was exhibited in Wright's work, Schindler, typically, carried it further than did Wright. As historian Neil Levine has discussed, except for a few examples, Wright seems mostly to have used diagonal planning only for personal or family projects, such as Taliesin (1911), in his early work.[35] Even in Taliesin, however, although there is a corner fireplace in one of the living spaces, the hipped roof restates the orthogonal axis rather than emphasizing the more dynamic diagonal one. Corner windows also appear in Wright; but, for example at his Freeman House in Los Angeles (1924–25), while the living room is entered at the corner and there are prominent corner windows, the central fireplace, which faces large glazed doors, establishes the room's symmetry around an orthogonal axis.[36] In contrast, at Schindler's 1925 How House, the living room is entered at the corner and the fireplace is connected to the opposite corner with built-in furniture; on the perpendicular diagonal axis, corner windows are at each end and the exposed roof framing is a series of double cantilevers that emphasize the diagonal (fig. 29a, b).

In Schindler's work, virtually all of the fireplaces are placed in the corners of rooms. The few exceptions include those in the S.P.G. and M.D.C. studios in the Kings Road house; when Schindler did place a fireplace at the center of a space, it was a lightweight metal one, such as the copper ones at Kings Road or the central aluminum and steel one at the Tischler House. This is in contrast to Wright's heavy hearths, as at the Robie House (1906–8).

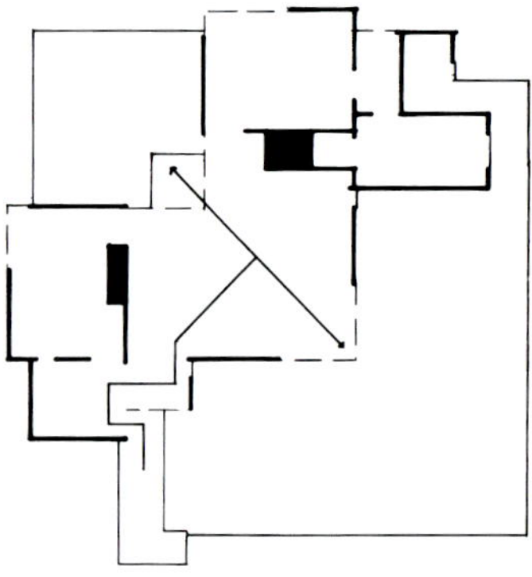

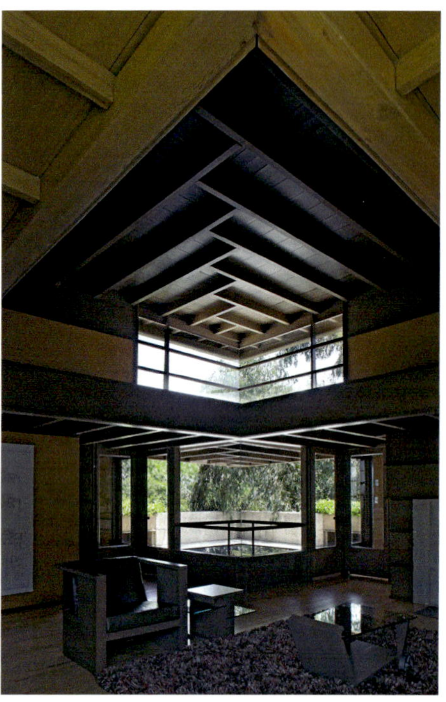

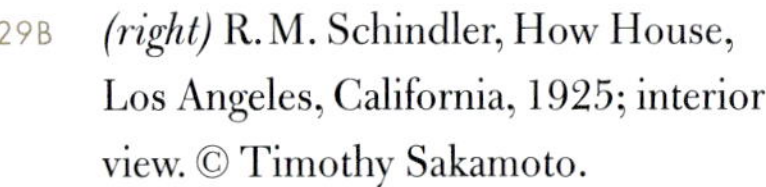

29A *(above)* R. M. Schindler, How House, Los Angeles, California, 1925; plan diagram. Drawing by Robert Alexander. This and subsequent diagrams are in the collection of Judith Sheine.

29B *(right)* R. M. Schindler, How House, Los Angeles, California, 1925; interior view. © Timothy Sakamoto.

While Schindler makes use of Wright's entry pattern, with a low vestibule leading to a higher living space, the Schindler houses emphasize diagonal movement in a far more dynamic way. In the Kings Road house, each L-shaped wing is entered from a small, low vestibule that looks out through a corner window into the previously hidden garden, and one moves through the rooms diagonally, largely from corner to corner, with corner fireplaces in the R. M. S. and C. B. C. studios, as well as in the outside patios (fig. 30a).[37] Numerous Schindler houses display these spatial characteristics, including the Oliver (1933–34; fig. 30b), Buck (1934; fig. 30c), and Rodriguez (1940–42; fig. 30d) houses, which are L shapes around patios or a garden, as well as the Wolfe House (1928–29; fig. 30e), in which each L-shaped level wraps around a corner balcony. Even in houses that do not have an L-shaped plan, diagonal axes, fireplaces, and corner windows are virtually always in evidence.

There are several other spatial patterns to be found in Schindler's buildings. Beginning with the Kings Road house, Schindler used a three-dimensional 4-foot grid to design—and build—his projects. Schindler's article "Reference Frames in Space" was published in 1946 (though he had written it in 1932).[38] The article describes the proportional system he had been using since Kings Road, one in which the 4-foot modules are broken into one-third units of 16 inches each. He justifies this system by its relation to human proportions (aesthetics), by its usefulness in visually laying out a building for construction purposes, and by its conformance with standard construction-material dimensions (4 × 8 foot panels,

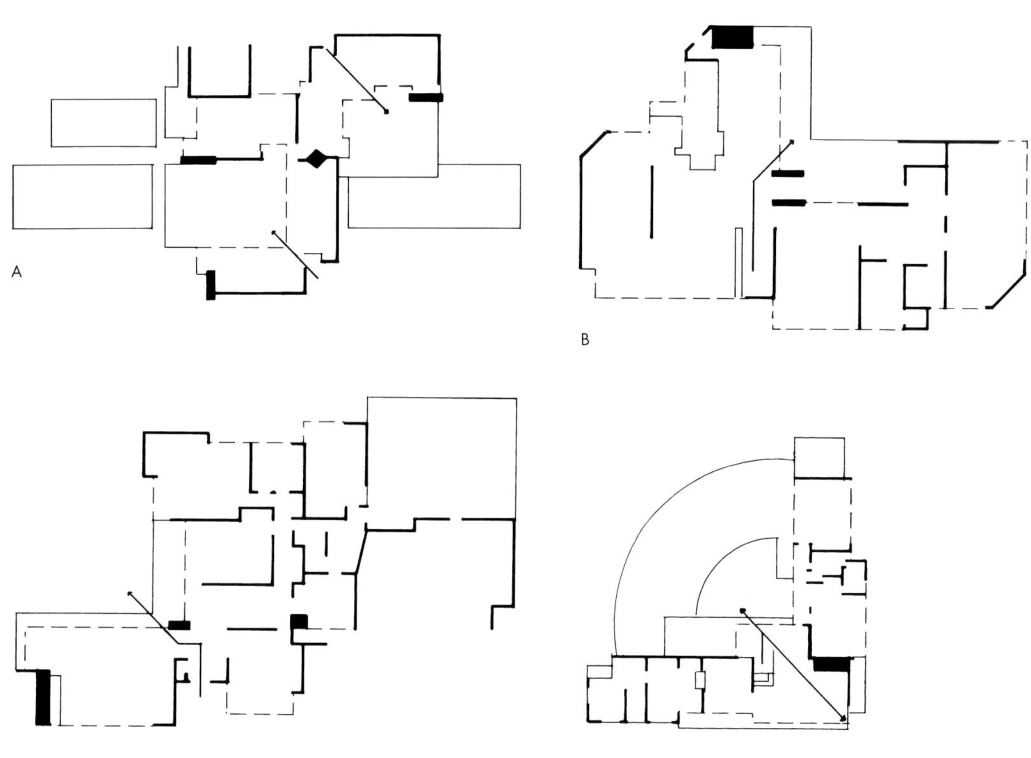

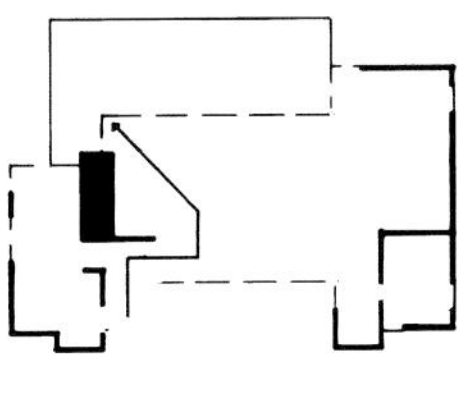

30A Plan diagram of the Kings Road house. Drawing by Robert Alexander.

30B Plan diagram of the Oliver House, Los Angeles, California, 1933–34. Drawing by Robert Alexander.

30C Plan diagram of the Buck House, Los Angeles, California, 1934. Drawing by Robert Alexander.

30D Plan diagram of the Rodriguez House, Los Angeles, California, 1940–42. Drawing by Robert Alexander.

30E Plan diagram of the Wolfe House, Avalon, Catalina Island, California, 1928–29. Drawing by Robert Alexander.

2 × 4 inch studs, etc.). It was a visual system that allowed the space architect to tie together all the parts of a design without having to add up a string of unrelated dimensions.

In 1947, Schindler published "The Schindler Frame," which described the modification of the wood-frame construction system he had introduced after World War II.[39] While it was ostensibly a technical article, Schindler actually described how best to establish the sectional spatial characteristics of Space Architecture, ones he had been developing in his work throughout his career. The major change Schindler made to the conventional wood-frame system was in cutting the standard 8-foot-high wood studs to 6 feet 8 inches or door height (1⅔ modules). This allowed for a continuous structural plate at that height that also formed a horizontal datum, a line that acted as a continuous visual reference. The datum served to tie the spaces together and allowed ceiling heights above the datum to vary, with clerestory windows between the roof and the datum. Although Wright had used a horizontal datum and clerestory windows in his early work, Schindler used the datum more extensively and dramatically, both structurally and spatially, in every project to unite interior spaces and to emphasize the house's connection to exterior spaces.[40] He manipulated the section to provide for spatial hierarchy, but also to allow light to come in from unexpected places; major spaces in a house had light coming in from three or four directions. The Kings Road house exhibited the horizontal datum, the large areas of glazing, the varied section (fig. 31a), the clerestory windows, the large overhangs, and the proximity of the floor to the ground that were to appear in later Schindler works and were codified as the desirable characteristics for Space Architecture in "The Schindler Frame." These sectional characteristics appear in numerous and varied ways in Schindler's work throughout his career: in the How House (fig. 31b), with its dramatic section along a diagonal axis; in Plaster-Skin works, such as the Oliver House (fig. 31c), which had a modified gable roof, and the Walker House (fig. 31d), with a double-sloping roof; and in Schindler Frame houses, including the Kallis House (fig. 31e), with its sloping roof and walls, and the Tischler House (fig. 31f), with its blue translucent gable.

In addition to setting the pattern for his own work and being a significant precedent for much of the Modern residential architecture in Southern California and elsewhere from the 1920s through the 1960s, the Kings Road house influenced a generation of Postmodern architects and continues to exert an influence on current practitioners. As a young architect, Frank Gehry visited the house and met Schindler; the exposed wood framing and the improvisational and experimental nature of Kings Road can certainly be seen in his work—particularly in his own house in Santa Monica (1978; fig. 32). Frank Israel's office was in the Kings Road house's enclosed carport from 1984 to 1986, and he often spoke about

31A Section of the Kings Road house. Drawing by Dino Parenti and Kenneth Todd.

31B Section of the How House. Drawing by Jin Ho Shin.

31C Section of the Oliver House. Drawing by Bach-Mai Cao and Stephen Thorlin.

31D Section of the Walker House, Los Angeles, California, 1935. Drawing by Tim Hall.

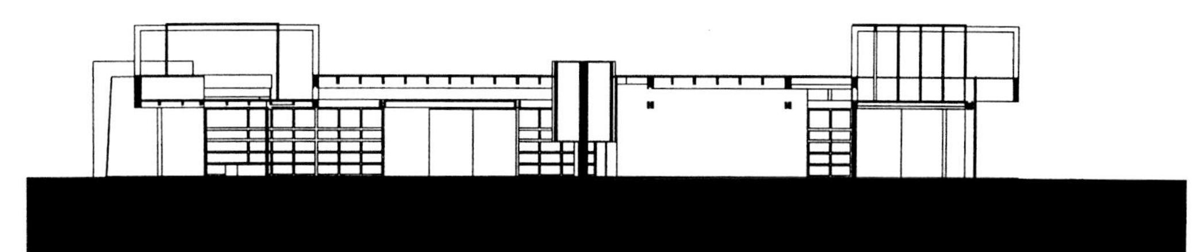
A

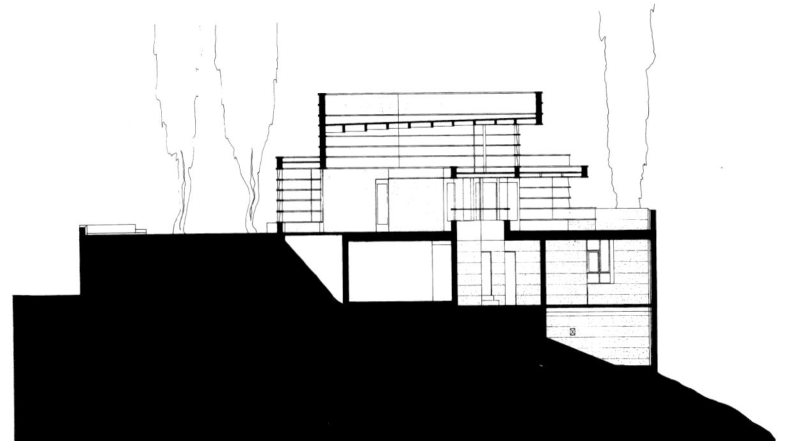
B

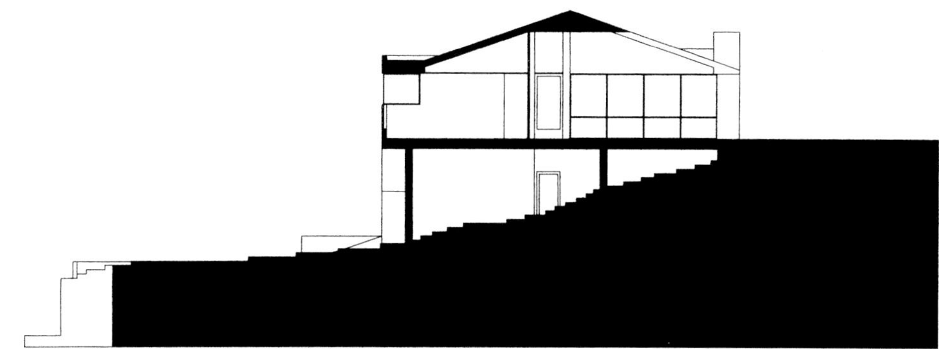
C

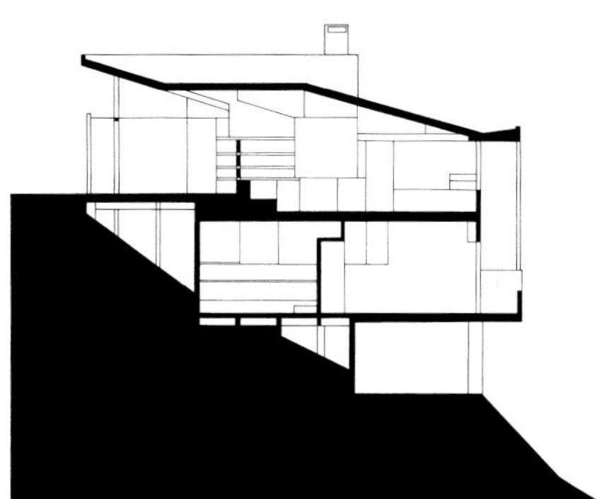
D

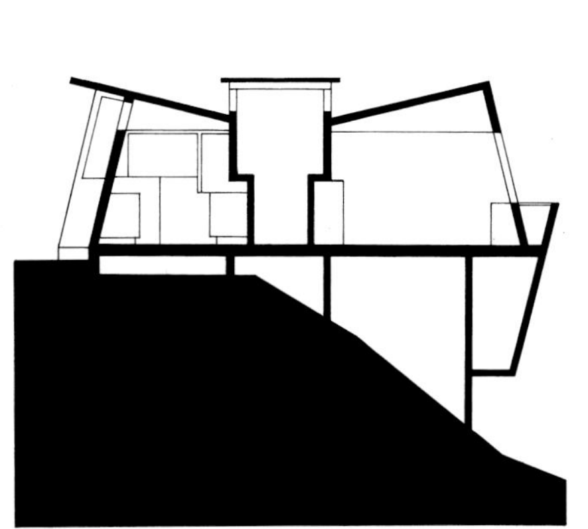

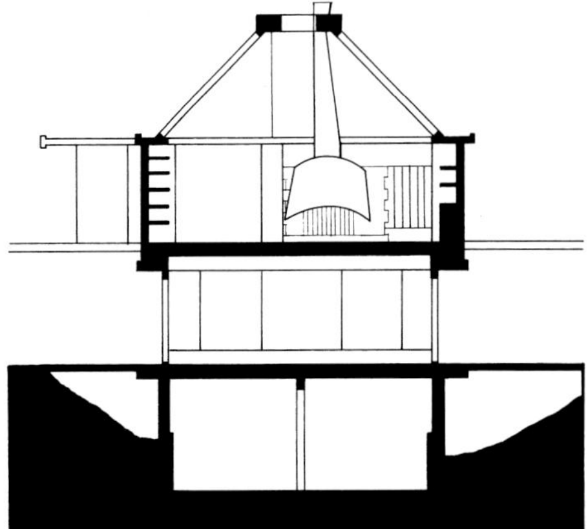

31E Section of the Kallis House. Drawing by Wendy Dailey.

31F Section of the Tischler House. Drawing by Wendy Dailey.

Schindler's work and its influence on his own. Michael Rotondi, who grew up in Silver Lake in Los Angeles, surrounded by Schindler buildings, admired Schindler's sensitivity to context and human scale. Schindler's "variety" was no longer seen as disadvantageous to a generation (or two) that embraced Robert Venturi's *Complexity and Contradiction in Architecture* (1966), in which he turned Mies van der Rohe's famous aphorism, "Less is more," into the Postmodern slogan, "Less is a bore."[41]

And for younger practitioners, Schindler and the Kings Road house still have something to offer. Schindler's sensitivity to site and climate extended to a detailed understanding of the unique characteristics of his adopted home. In an unpublished article from 1944 called "Notes: Modern Architecture," Schindler wrote:

> Southern California is a completely unique corner of the U.S.A. Although in a tropical latitude, its climate is definitely not tropical. Its flora is not tropical nor has it real desert characteristics. Its slight seasonal variations lead to a relaxed outdoor life of especial ease. Although its sun is strong, it is controlled by morning fogs. The resulting character of light and color are unique. Instead of the opaque material coloring of the east, we have here subtle transparent shades created by the light on grayish backgrounds.[42]

Schindler's indoor-outdoor designs incorporated cross-ventilation, overhangs to provide shade, and extensive use of natural light, all of which minimized the need for heating, cooling, and artificial illumination; they are models for sustainable design, as were his construction practices, which maximized the efficient use of materials.

The Kings Road house also serves as a model for low-cost, Modern prefabricated designs, which are of interest again to current practitioners. For example, Marmol Radziner's

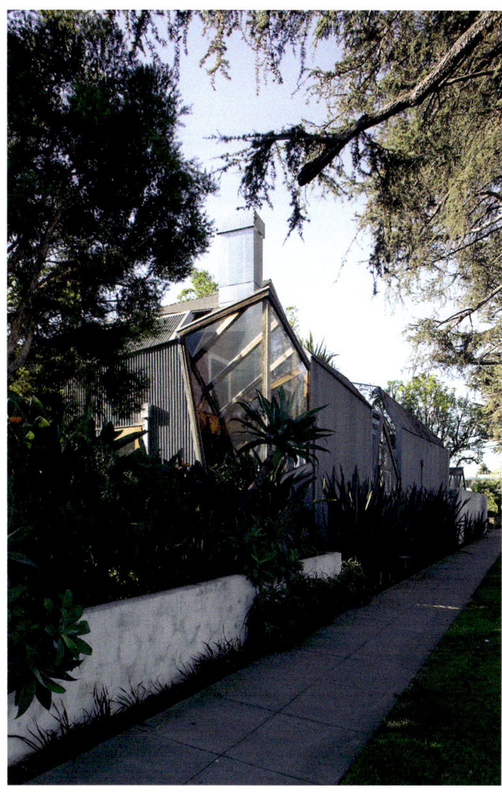

32 Frank Gehry, Gehry House, Santa Monica, California, 1978. © Timothy Sakamoto.

modular, factory-built Modern houses, with their flat roofs, expansive areas of glass and overhangs, and their emphasis on indoor-outdoor living (fig. 33), pay homage to Kings Road, with its modular, systematized construction.[43] The new prefab designs are taking advantage of file-to-factory processes enabled by advances in digital design and fabrication, but even there, Schindler set a precedent. The three-dimensional 4-foot grid is a form of parameterization that lends itself to digital processes, including minimizing waste in construction materials.[44] And for several other current trends, including a focus on the integration of architecture and landscape and alternative practices such as design-build, Schindler could be seen as precedent-setting. He designed landscape as an integral part of his buildings and he acted as his own contractor, first at Kings Road and then widely in his practice.

But whatever precedents the Kings Road house set, none of them may be as important as its inherent worth as a piece of architectural design. The Kings Road house was Schindler's most personal work and, in many ways, his most satisfying. For Schindler, Kings Road may have been the most perfect example of Space Architecture—in part, at least, because it was for the most perfect client: himself. The house has proved to be timeless, which is what Schindler would have most wished for it. He saw himself as a classicist and the Kings Road house as his most representative building.[45] In 1952 he wrote to Esther McCoy about how he saw his career and his house:

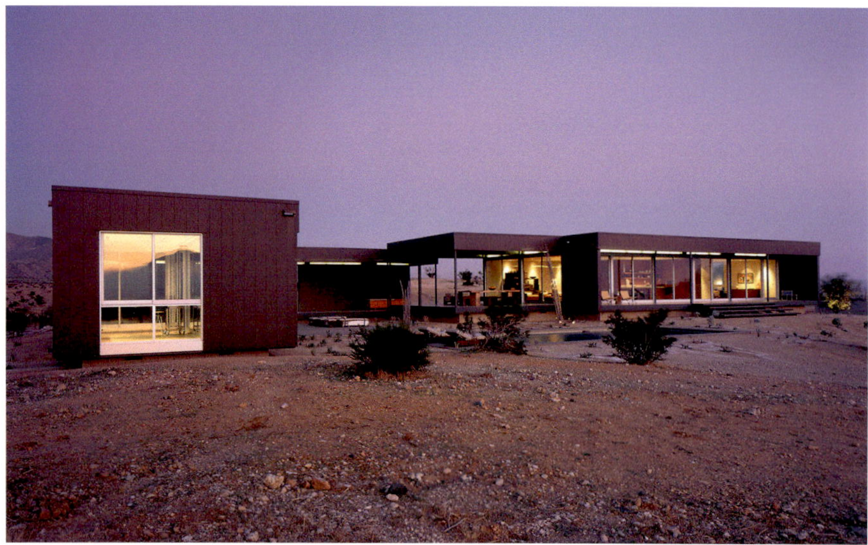

33 Marmol Radziner, Desert House, Desert Hot Springs, California, 2005. © Benny Chan/ Fotoworks.

> Yes the romantic writer fastens unto a few traits of life and balloons them without sence of balance & reality into a world of his own. The classiker lets say like "Proust" however carefully digs into the mass of life material until slowly and painstaingingly some of the woof and warf of reality starts to reappear shining through his canvass.[46]

Schindler dismissed both Wright and Neutra as romantics, as well as practitioners of the International Style in general, declaring:

> So finally there is only the classicist left—"me."
>
> I came to live & work in California. I camped under the open sky, in the redwoods, on the beach, the foothills & the desert. I tested its adobe its granite & its sky. And out of a carefully built up conception of how the human being could grow roots in this soil—unique & delightful—I built my house.
>
> And unless I failed it should be as Californian as the Parthenon is Greek and the Forum Roman. In fact the beginning of a new "classic" growth drinking California sap.

Apparently, though, Schindler did not fail. The Kings Road house is increasingly recognized as being central to the development of twentieth-century architecture and as a precedent-setting masterpiece.[47] We can only hope that the house will continue to be the model for the best of Southern California architecture.

APPENDIX LETTERS

LETTER FROM R. M. SCHINDLER TO ESTHER McCOY IN MEXICO

February 18, 1952
Handwritten

I am still in the hospital (4 weeks)—with two very close gropings towards the shadows—but finally hope that another week will free me.

And enough energy now to argue with you on classicism. Maybe the terms would clear if we remember the third point of the triangle the "academic". Yes the romantic writer fastens unto a few traits of life and balloons them without sence of balance & reality into a world of his own. The classiker lets say like "Proust" however carefully digs into the mass of life material until slowly & painstaingingly some of the woof and warf of reality starts to reappear shining through his canvass.

Frank Lloyd Wright is a romantiker if after a few months visit with Japanese officials he builds his "Imperial Hotel" a brilliant composition of bits of tradition, present struggles & future aspirations gathered at random, but with a very slim [?] seasoning of Japanese character & life. It will remain a sterile beautiful castle in the air.

Or whan he comes to built his California house & tries to get it "into character" by accepting a few sculpturaral forms originated by a people who likely came across the Bearing See *[sic]* and trekked down the coast to Mexico apparently never noticing that the[y] past California on their way.

And so is Neutra who arrives from Europe on the wings of the "International Style"—reflecting that since th[e] cows dung will benefit any piece of ground it drops on starts trying to build houses supposedly being exa[c]tly the same as his comrades in theory and style are designing in Germany, France & South America.

And last of all the "Abstract School" which arranges geometric shapes in patch quilt fashion romantically thinking that a whole "an organism—which a house must be" can be achieved by mathematical addition of life less parts which never get a[c]quainted with each other. (Kinder garten chains).

No—each of these parts must suddenly realize that they are becoming part of a whole and architecture starts as soon as the architect is able to give them life & strength to drop their geometric cocoon and take their place as individ[u]al, related & harmoniously tuned members of the orchestra.

So finally there is only the classicist left—"me."

I came to live & work in California. I camped under the open sky, in the redwoods, on the beach, the foot hills & the desert. I tested its adobe its granite & its sky. And out of a carefully built up conception of how the human being could grow roots in this soil—unique & delightful—I built my house.

And unless I failed it should be as Californian as the Parthenon is Greek and the Forum Roman. In fact the beginning of a new "classic" growth drinking California sap.

This does not eliminate individual expression. Every building on the Parthenon bears the stamp of its creator. But it raises the spectre of the "academic" the professor easely boils of[f] the flesh and distributes the skeleton as an easy substitute for the quick & the blind.

Forgive this wordiness but last night was long & sleepless and the hospital a horror.

RMS

LETTER FROM R. M. SCHINDLER TO ESTHER McCOY IN MEXICO

March 5, 1952
Handwritten

Yes—I am back at work but only a few hours a day—still very easely tired—it will probably take a few more months to recuperate fully.

I am cutting down on my work and somewhat uncertain what to do in the future—whatever that is. I feel like I had left an old house to enter a new room—small, circumscribed, with bare walls and only one exit. Coming to Mexico is a wish without shape too.

RMS

Credit: Both letters are in the Rudolph M. Schindler Collection, Architecture and Design Collection, Art, Design & Architecture Museum, University of California, Santa Barbara.

NOTES

INTRODUCTION

1. The architectural achievements of the Schindler House are well documented through the writings of Judith Sheine, Lionel March, Michael Darling, Elizabeth Smith, and the curator of early Modernism in Southern California, Esther McCoy.

2. As Robert Sweeney's essay illustrates in vivid colors.

3. Initiated by Peter Noever, director of the Österreichisches Museum für Angewandte Kunst (Austrian Museum of Applied Arts), Vienna (MAK), from 1986 to 2011, the Republic of Austria entered into a cooperation agreement with Friends of the Schindler House (FOSH) in 1994 to hold exhibits and other cultural programs at the house under the auspices of the MAK Center for Art and Architecture at the Schindler House.

PRÉCIS

1. Richard J. Neutra, *Wie Baut Amerika?* (Stuttgart: Julius Hoffmann, 1927). The English title is *How America Builds?* In 1985, Johnson was quoted as saying, "How I got to Schindler's Kings Road House, I don't remember. . . . His original house, being cut in two and being cramped and crabbed and difficult, really was horrible." Kazys Varnelis, ed., *The Philip Johnson Tapes: Interviews by Robert A. M. Stern* (New York: The Monacelli Press, 2008), 42–43.

2. R. M. Schindler, "A Cooperative Dwelling," *T-Square* 2 (February 1932): 20–21. "The California House: 1922," *Los Angeles Times,* July 19, 1953.

3. Esther McCoy, "R. M. Schindler, 1887–1953," in *Five California Architects* (New York: Reinhold Publishing, 1960), 156–60.

4. R. M. Schindler, "Contribution for the Directory on Contemporary Architecture Collected by the School of Architecture, University of Southern California, by R. M. Schindler, Architect, 1949," in "R. M. Schindler, Architect," a privately circulated mimeograph, no pp.; in the possession of Robert Sweeney. Copies of this ephemeral publication are in the collections of the Architecture and Design Collection, Art, Design & Architecture Museum, University of California, Santa Barbara; and the Getty Research Institute, Los Angeles, California. Schindler's brief introductory statement is dated June 1948.

5. Pauline Schindler to Sophie Gibling, May 9, 1916, in the Schindler family's possession.

6. Following up in 1988, Johnson stated, "I've still never seen his work. But I realize now my mistake. This man was an artist." Philip Johnson to Robert Sweeney, personal communication, New York, June 23, 1988. Published in *MAK Center for Art and Architecture: R. M. Schindler,* edited by Peter Noever for MAK, Vienna, and MAK Center for Art and Architecture (Los Angeles, Munich, and New York: Prestel, 1995), 38.

THE KINGS ROAD HOUSE ROBERT SWEENEY

Unless otherwise noted, all correspondence cited is held by the Schindler family. R. M. Schindler is identified as RMS; Sophie Pauline Gibling Schindler is identified as SPG; Sophie S. Gibling (Pauline's mother) is identified as SSG; Edmund J. Gibling (Pauline's father) is identified as EJG; and Dorothy S. Gibling (Pauline's younger sister) is identified as DSG. Events took an unexpected turn in March 1922: with apparent suddenness, Pauline accepted a teaching job at Central Union High School in El Centro, then an agricultural backwater in Imperial County. The correspondence does not clarify her motives, though a sly comment by Schindler suggests that all was not well in Los Angeles. Nonetheless, her absence resulted in a detailed written history of the construction of the Kings Road house that we probably would not have otherwise. Some correspondence is in the Frank Lloyd Wright/R. M. Schindler Collection at the Getty Research Institute for the History of Art and the Humanities, Los Angeles; it is identified as GRI. Other documents and letters are from the Schindler Papers in the Architecture and Design Collection (identified as ADC), Art, Design & Architecture Museum, University of California, Santa Barbara.

1. The official document granting and presumably explaining the name change was destroyed in a fire during World War II. Jews in Vienna often changed their names at this time to escape anti-Semitism. If that was the case, the new surname Schindler did not entirely address the issue.

2. Markus Kristan, *Carl König 1841–1915: Ein neubarocker Großstadtarchitekt in Wien* (Vienna: Verlag Holzhausen, 1999), 147. English translation is by Markus Kristan.

3. Kristan, *Carl König,* 147.

4. Carl E. Schorske, "Otto Wagner," in *Macmillan Encyclopedia of Architects,* ed. Adolf K. Placzek (New York: The Free Press; and London: Collier Macmillan, 1982), 358.

5. Records of k.k. Akademie der bildenden Künst, Vienna. Schindler Papers, ADC.

6. RMS to Adolf Loos, n.d. RMS to Louis Sullivan, August 26, 1920. Both in Esther McCoy, *Vienna to Los Angeles: Two Journeys* (Santa Monica, Calif.: Arts and Architecture Press, 1979), 143. According to Esther McCoy, Schindler and Sullivan met at Taliesin.

7. *Der Architekt,* supplement no. 7 (1900).

8. "Er hat unter anderen Arbeiten die selbstständige Bauleitung eines grossen, und technisch sehr komplicierten Baues (das Haus des österreich. Bühnenverein, Wien I. Doroteergasse 6 & 8) zu unserer vollsten Zufriedenheit durchgeführt. Wir sehen ihm mit dem grössten Bedauern aus unserem Atelier scheiden." Hans Mayr to ——, February 20, 1914. Schindler Papers, ADC.

9. "Amerika," print advertisement, source unknown, November 8, 1913. Schindler Papers, ADC.

10. Ellis Island Records. RMS to Richard Neutra, Chicago, March 1914, in McCoy, *Vienna to Los Angeles,* 104.

11. RMS to Frank Lloyd Wright, n.d., but Wright's response establishes the month of November. GRI, Box 1, folder 3.

12. Wright's letter is not dated, but the envelope is postmarked December 10. Harry F. Robinson to Mrs. Avery Coonley, December 30, 1914. Frank Lloyd Wright, *An Autobiography* (London, New York, and Toronto: Longmans Green, 1932), 164. Frank Lloyd Wright to Miss Kimbell, Miss Hazelton, and Miss Wigginton, October 20, 1917. GRI, Box 1, folder 3.

13. Frank Lloyd Wright to RMS, n.d., GRI, Box 1, folder 5.

14. Robert Winter, interview with Pauline Schindler, 1975; in possession of Friends of the Schindler House.

15. "Radicals Have Split Socialist Congress," *New York Times,* September 1, 1919. "Force Communists to Remove Flags," *New York Times,* September 2, 1919. "Form Red Party; Leader Arrested," *New York Times,* September 3, 1919. "New Party Raises Bolshevist Banner," *New York Times,* September 4, 1919. "The Communist Party," *New York Times,* September 5, 1919. SPG to SSG and EJG, n.d.

16. SPG to Ruth Imogene Theberath, September 25, 1920. Frank Lloyd Wright to RMS, September 9, [1919], GRI, Box 1, folder 11.

17. Frank Lloyd Wright to RMS, February 9, 1920. GRI, Box 1, folder 14.

18. Wire, RMS to Frank Lloyd Wright, April 17, 1920. Wire, Frank Lloyd Wright to RMS, April 26, [1920]. Both GRI, Box 1, folder 16.

19. Galka Scheyer coined the aphorism "bold and novel construction" to describe the architecture she encountered in Los Angeles in 1925; she specifically mentioned Schindler and Neutra, "students of Wright," and H. Sachs, "more for interior design." Isabel Wünsche, ed., *Galka E. Scheyer & the Blue Four: Correspondence 1924–1945* (Wabern and Bern: Benteli Verlags, 2006), 95.

20. SPG to ——, December 3, 6, 1920. SPG to ——, December 19, 1920. SPG to Beloved Parients, Wednesday, January 1921.

21. SPG to Beloved People, Saturday, July 1921. Marian Da Camara Chace to SPG, January 15, 1921. SPG to People, August 25, 1921. SPG to SSG, November 11, 1921.

22. RMS to EJG, December 16, 1921.

23. SPG to EJG, November 16, 1921.

24. RMS to ——, December 16, 1921.

25. R.M. Schindler, "A Cooperative Dwelling." *T-Square* 2 (February 1932): 20.

26. RMS to ——, January 4, 1922. SPG to Mother, Saturday evening [February 13, 1922].

27. Sophie to [SPG] ——, Sunday evening [February 20, 1922].

28. RMS to [SPG], n.d. [envelope postmarked March 7, 1922]. RMS to [SPG], Saturday [March 11, 1922].

29. RMS to ——, March 15, 1921 [*sic:* 1922]. RMS to EJG, March 16, [1922].

30. RMS to SPG, n.d. [envelope postmarked April 14, 1922]. RMS to SPG, n.d. [envelope postmarked April 20, 1922]. RMS to SPG, n.d. [envelope dated April 22, 1922].

31. RMS to SPG, March 20, [1922]. RMS to [SPG], Monday.

32. SPG to SSG, Sunday [March 26, 1922]. RMS to [SPG], Monday.

33. SPG to Parients, April 25, [1922]. DSG to ——, Saturday [August 5, 1922].

34. RMS to ——, June 26, 1922.

35. Schindler, "A Cooperative Dwelling," 21.

36. Schindler, "A Cooperative Dwelling," 20–21.

37. DSG to ——, Monday [July 31, 1922]. DSG to ——, August 11, 1922.

38. SPG to SSG, Wednesday [October 29, 1924].

39. DSG to [SSG, EJG], 22 [April 1923]. For a detailed discussion of social activity at the Schindler House in the early years, see Robert Sweeney, "Life at Kings Road: As It Was, 1920–1940," in *The Architecture of R. M. Schindler,* ed. Elizabeth A. T. Smith and Michael Darling (Los Angeles: The Museum of Contemporary Art, and New York: Harry N. Abrams, 2001), 86–115.

40. Robert Winter, interview with Pauline Schindler, 1975; in possession of Friends of the Schindler House.

THE KINGS ROAD HOUSE: PRE-EVERYBODY JUDITH SHEINE

Unless otherwise noted, the source for all documents and correspondence is the Rudolph M. Schindler Collection, Architecture and Design Collection, Art, Design & Architecture Museum, University of California, Santa Barbara. R. M. Schindler is identified as RMS.

1. Schindler published an article in 1944 on the role of the architect in the building industry: "Architect—Postwar—Post Everybody," *Pencil Points* 25 (October 1944): 16–18 and (November 1944): 12–14. In it Schindler lamented that the architect had little control over the building process and, in fact, got paid after all the other participants in the design process, i.e., post-everybody. For the Kings Road house, Schindler was the architect, landscape architect, engineer, interior designer, and contractor. Here, payment would not have been much of an issue; the house served as a precedent for so much of the Modern architecture that followed that, at least in this case, the architect could be said to be pre-everybody.

2. Reyner Banham, *Age of the Masters: A Personal View of Modern Architecture* (New York: Harper & Row, 1975), 158–59.

3. Letter from RMS to Richard Neutra, Los Angeles, June 16, 1922, published in Esther McCoy, *Vienna to Los Angeles: Two Journeys* (Santa Monica, Calif.: Arts and Architecture Press, 1979), 139–40.

4. Letter from Louis Sullivan to RMS, July 18, 1922. At the time, Sullivan was corresponding with Schindler, in part as Frank Lloyd Wright's representative, and also to try to track down a typed manuscript of Sullivan's, "Kindergarten Chats," which Schindler had been trying to help get published in Europe.

5. A section is a vertical slice taken through a building, showing the heights and configurations of the floors and ceilings. Adolf Loos's work was characterized by sections showing many levels of floors and ceilings, sometimes with several different floor and ceiling heights within a room or in adjacent rooms. Schindler's work was influenced by Loos's ideas about interior space, and also exhibited complex sections.

6. Schindler dated this document 1912; however, there is a handwritten copy in German dated 1913. All quotes are from Schindler's own translation of this document into English, ca. 1932.

7. For a more detailed discussion of Schindler's manifesto and its sources, see Judith Sheine, *R. M. Schindler* (New York and London: Phaidon Press, 2001).

8. Schindler wrote about these ideas, and many others to be found in his later writings, in his notes for a series of lectures he gave at the Church School in Chicago in 1916.

9. Published in Berlin by Verlag Ernst Wasmuth in 1911. The English title is *Studies and Executed Buildings by Frank Lloyd Wright.*

10. Schindler also worked with three Japanese architects—Arata Endo, Goichi Fujikura, and Kameki Tsuchiura—who were already working for Wright at Taliesin and in Chicago when he joined Wright's office in February 1918. See Kathryn Smith, *Frank Lloyd Wright: Hollyhock House and Olive Hill* (New York: Rizzoli, 1992), 23.

11. While courtyards and patios were common in both European and Southern California architecture, Schindler's use of them in the Kings Road house, making them virtually continuous with the interior space, was new, as was treating them as essentially the main living rooms of the house.

12. Smith, *Frank Lloyd Wright,* 94; Kathryn Smith, "The Schindler House," in *R. M. Schindler: Composition and Construction,* ed. Lionel March and Judith Sheine (London: Academy Editions, 1993), 115. In the earlier book, Smith cited the footprints of two unbuilt projects at Olive Hill as precedents for the one at Kings Road—the original design for the director's house (1920) and the

design of an apartment building for actors (1920)—but concluded that Schindler, not Wright, was certainly responsible for the design of the latter and probably for the specific footprint of the former.

13. Lionel March, *Rudolph M. Schindler: R. M. Schindler House, Hollywood, California, 1921–22; James E. How House, Los Angeles, California, 1925* (Tokyo: A.D.A. Edita, 1999).

14. RMS to Neutra, June 16, 1922, in McCoy, *Vienna to Los Angeles,* 139–40.

15. Pueblo Ribera Court was published in Bruno Taut, *Bauen* (1927), 56; Bruno Taut, *Bauen der Neue Wohnbau* (1927), 114–16; *Architectural Record* 67 (July 1930): 17–21; and *Western Architect* 39 (August 1930): 117, 118. The How House was published in *Das Neue Frankfurt* (1928); *Architectural Record* 65 (1929): 5–9; Bruno Taut, *Die Neue Baukunst in Europa and Amerika* (Stuttgart: Julius Hoffman, 1929), 178–79; *Pyramide* (1929); and Richard Neutra, *Amerika* (Vienna: Anton Schroll, 1930), 130–32. The Lovell Beach House was published in *Popular Mechanics Magazine* 48 (June 1927): 969; *Architectural Record* 66 (September 1929); and Neutra, *Amerika,* 139.

16. Letter from RMS to Maxwell Levinson, dated January 20, 1931, but possibly written in January 1932 and misdated; Schindler was presumably referring to Mies's model house in the 1931 Berlin Building Exposition.

17. *T-Square* 2 (February 1932).

18. Letter from RMS to Richard Neutra, Los Angeles, December 1920 or January 1921, published in translation in August Sarnitz, *R. M. Schindler, Architect 1887–1953* (New York: Rizzoli, 1988), 205. This letter described Schindler's assessment of American architecture after nearly six years in the United States.

19. This work included the Barnsdall House, which Schindler had worked on (a project that had brought him to Southern California), as well as the concrete block houses: Millard (1923), Storer (1923), Freeman (1924), and Ennis (1924). In "Contribution for the Directory on Contemporary Architecture Collected by the School of Architecture, University of Southern California, by R. M. Schindler, Architect, 1949" (with a brief introductory statement dated June 1948), he wrote that the Wright buildings at Olive Hill, which included the Barnsdall House, employed "Mayan motifs." This commentary is included in "R. M. Schindler, Architect," a privately circulated mimeograph; copies are in the collections of the Architecture and Design Collection, Art, Design & Architecture Museum, University of California, Santa Barbara; and the Getty Research Institute, Los Angeles.

20. The first Wright Usonian design has been identified as the 1933 Lusk House. See Pamela D. Kingsbury, *Frank Lloyd Wright and Wichita: The First Usonian Design* (Wichita, Kans.: Wichita-Sedgwick County Historical Museum, 1992).

21. Letter published in *Architectural Forum* 87, no. 2 (August 1947): 22.

22. Esther McCoy worked for Schindler as a draftsperson in the 1940s and subsequently published a number of articles about his work that appeared in the architectural press in the 1950s before the publication of her *Five California Architects* (New York: Reinhold, 1960).

23. Reyner Banham wrote about Schindler a number of times; see above, *Age of the Masters,* and especially *Los Angeles: The Architecture of Four Ecologies* (New York: Harper & Row, 1971). Hans Hollein published "R. M. Schindler: Ein Weiner Architekt in Kalifornien," *Der Aufbau* 16, no. 3 (March 1961): 102–4 and "Rudolf M. Schindler: Ein weiterer Beitrag zur Berichtigung der Architeckturgeschichte," *Bau* 21, no. 4 (1966): 67–82. Herman Hertzberger wrote "Dedicato a Schindler," *Domus* 465 (September 1967): 2–7. David Gebhard, *Schindler* (London: Thames and Hudson, 1971).

24. R. M. Schindler, "Space Architecture," *Dune Forum* (February 1934): 44–46.

25. Henry-Russell Hitchcock and Philip Johnson, *The International Style: Architecture since 1922* (New York: W. W. Norton, 1966; orig. 1932).

26. For a detailed discussion of this exhibit and the decisions about which architects to include and why, see Terence Riley, *The International Style: Exhibition 15 and the Museum of Modern Art* (New York: Rizzoli, 1992).

27. Henry-Russell Hitchcock, *Modern Architecture: Romanticism and Reintegration* (New York: Da Capo Press, 1993; orig. 1929). Hitchcock was not very complimentary in his brief discussion of Schindler's work in the text. Schindler, for his part, questioned Hitchcock's interest in three-dimensional architecture, objecting to Hitchcock's use only of photographs to illustrate works, without showing plans and sections, which Schindler thought would give a better understanding of the presented architecture. Hitchcock replied with a dismissive letter indicating that he was more interested in European work than American and that if any work drew him to California, it would be Neutra's.

28. Letter from RMS to Philip Johnson, March 9, 1932.

29. The Janson House has blue translucent fiberglass walls and the Tischler House has a blue translucent fiberglass gable roof. The Skolnik House, with half of a gable roof at its center made of translucent fiberglass, was not finished until later, in 1952. Schindler may have referred to these houses as "a final development" because he had been diagnosed with cancer at the end of 1951 and by 1952 was likely thinking that the end of his career was near. Letter from RMS to Arthur Drexler, April 12, 1952.

30. Schindler experimented with a number of concrete-forming techniques designed to conserve on formwork and cost. These included the Slab-Tilt system employed at Kings Road; the Slab-Cast system, in which one board height, or 16 inches, of concrete was poured each day and the formwork was moved up 16 inches and reused the next day (used in Pueblo Ribera Court [1923–25] and the How House [1925]); the Slab-Gun system, employing sprayed-on concrete, used in the Packard House (1924); movable formwork reused for each concrete frame, employed at the Lovell Beach House (1922–26); and concrete floors poured over corrugated iron formwork, used in the Wolfe House (1928–29) and the Elliot House (1930). Schindler referred to his concrete and exposed-wood construction methods as Structural-Core Design.

31. Schindler's Plaster-Skin Design work featured interlocking volumes, both inside and out, while displaying the horizontal datum, clerestory windows, and other features of his Space Architecture. Examples include the Oliver (1933–34), Buck (1934), Walker (1935), and Wilson (1935–39) houses.

32. Henry-Russell Hitchcock, "An Eastern Critic Looks at Western Architecture," *California Arts and Architecture* 57 (1940): 21–23, 40–41.

33. In this sense, Schindler adhered closely to Wright's notion of organic architecture as arising from the conditions on the site.

34. Examples of buildings with L-shaped plans include Buena Shore Club (1916–18) and the How, Wolfe (1928–29), Oliver (1933–34), Buck (1934), Kaun (1934–35), DeKeyser (1935), McAlmon (1935), Fitzpatrick (1936), Van Dekker (1939–40), Goodwin (1940–41), Druckman (1940–42), Droste (1940), Rodriguez (1940–42), Harris (1942), Presburger (1945–47), Armon (1946–49), and Skolnik (1950–52) houses.

35. Neil Levine, "Frank Lloyd Wright's Diagonal Planning," in *In Search of Modern Architecture: A Tribute to Henry-Russell Hitchcock*, ed. Helen Searing (New York and Cambridge, Mass.: The Architectural History Foundation/MIT Press, 1982), 245–47. Also Neil Levine, *The Architecture of Frank Lloyd Wright* (Princeton, N.J.: Princeton University Press, 1996), 148–89.

36. Schindler remodeled the Freeman House a number of times over the period from 1926 to 1952, largely using built-in and freestanding furniture to break up the bilateral symmetry of the original Wright design, particularly in the living room.

37. The C.B.C. studio is entered essentially in the middle, but the corner fireplace reemphasizes the diagonal.

38. R.M. Schindler, "Reference Frames in Space," *Architect and Engineer* 165 (April 1946): 10, 40, 42–43. For a detailed discussion of this system, see Lionel March, "'Proportion Is an Alive and Expressive Tool,'" in *R. M. Schindler: Composition and Construction,* ed. March and Sheine, 88–101.

39. R.M. Schindler, "The Schindler Frame," *Architectural Record* 101 (May 1947): 143–46. For a detailed discussion of this article see Judith Sheine, "Construction and the Schindler Frame," in *R.M. Schindler: Composition and Construction,* ed. March and Sheine, 228–51. The spatial characteristics that are outlined in this article can be summarized in seven points: (1) large openings in walls; (2) varying ceiling heights; (3) low horizontal datum; (4) clerestory windows; (5) large overhangs; (6) interior floor close to exterior ground; (7) continuity between adjoining "space units" (rooms). The Kings Road house displays points 1–6; point 7 can be seen only in the continuity between interior and exterior spaces, as the concrete wall panels, arranged in Ls and Us, separate the individual studios from one another.

40. In Kings Road, the horizontal datum is at 6 feet 2 inches. Schindler used 1-foot vertical divisions at Kings Road and the datum is six 1-foot divisions plus the 2-inch base. The datum was raised to 6 feet 8 inches in subsequent work.

41. Robert Venturi, *Complexity and Contradiction in Architecture* (New York: The Museum of Modern Art, 1966), 25. The phrase "Less is more," usually attributed to Mies van der Rohe, was actually first coined by Peter Behrens, in whose office Mies had been employed.

42. R.M. Schindler, "Notes: Modern Architecture," unpublished (1944). It should be noted, however, that living close to nature, even in the benign climate of Southern California, does require wearing a sweater indoors in what passes for winter, as well as spending as much time as possible in shaded outdoor spaces in the heat of the summer. Of course, that does tend to keep the heating and cooling costs down in a very sustainable manner.

43. Marmol Radziner Prefab; see their 2005 prototype, the Desert House, designed for principal Leo Marmol in Desert Hot Springs.

44. Parameterization is the use of prescribed numerical characteristics to define design constraints.

45. By "classicist" Schindler did not mean a return to classical architecture. He meant that the work would be timeless, that it would be the expression of a specific (vs. universal) culture, that it would be completely integrated into its site and respond to its climate. For a more detailed discussion of these ideas, see Sheine, *R. M. Schindler.*

46. Letter from RMS to Esther McCoy dated February 18, 1952. The entire letter is included in this publication.

47. In a recent *Los Angeles Times* survey of architects, preservationists, and academics, Schindler's Kings Road house was chosen as number 1 of the top ten houses in Southern California. See Sean Mitchell, "Their All-Time Favorite Houses," *Los Angeles Times,* December 27, 2008, Home section.

SELECTED BIBLIOGRAPHY

1932

Schindler, R. M. "A Cooperative Dwelling." *T-Square* (Philadelphia) 2 (February 1932): 20–21. Reprinted in August Sarnitz, *R. M. Schindler, Architect.* Vienna: Akademie der bildenden Künste; Vienna and Munich: Edition Christian Brandstätter, 1986, pp. 150–51; English edition: New York: Rizzoli, 1988, 49.

1947

Schindler, R. M. Letter to the editor. *Architectural Forum* 87, no. 2 (August 1947): 22.

1949

Schindler, R. M. "Contribution for the Directory on Contemporary Architecture Collected by the School of Architecture, University of Southern California, by R. M. Schindler, Architect, 1949." In "R. M. Schindler, Architect." Mimeograph, privately circulated, no pp. Copies of this ephemeral publication are in the collections of the Architecture and Design Collection, Art, Design & Architecture Museum, University of California, Santa Barbara; and the Getty Research Institute, Los Angeles. Schindler's brief introductory statement is dated June 1948.

1953

"The California House: 1922." *Los Angeles Times,* July 19, 1953.

McCoy, Esther. "4 Schindler Houses of the 1920's." *Arts & Architecture* 70, no. 9 (September 1953): 12, 31.

1960

McCoy, Esther. "R. M. Schindler, 1887–1953." In her *Five California Architects.* New York: Reinhold, 1960, pp. 156–60.

1967

Banham, Reyner. "Rudolph Schindler: A Pioneer without Tears." *Architectural Design* (London) 37, no. 12 (December 1967): 578–79.

Gebhard, David. *An Exhibition of the Architecture of R. M. Schindler (1887–1953): Organized by David Gebhard for Presentation at the Art Gallery, University of California, Santa Barbara, March 30 to April 30, 1967. The Los Angeles County Museum of Art, Fall 1967.* University of California, 1967, pp. 20, 61–62.

1971

Banham, Reyner. *Los Angeles: The Architecture of Four Ecologies.* New York: Harper & Row, 1971, pp. 182–84.

———. "The Master Builders: 5." *The Sunday Times Magazine* (London), August 8, 1971.

Gebhard, David. *Schindler,* preface by Henry-Russell Hitchcock. London: Thames and Hudson, 1971, pp. 47–51. Other editions: New York: Viking Press, 1972; Santa Barbara: Peregrine Smith, Inc., 1980; San Francisco: William Stout Publishers, 1997.

1975

Banham, Reyner. "Schindler/Chase *[sic]* House, Los Angeles." In his *Age of the Masters: A Personal View of Modern Architecture.* New York: Harper & Row, 1975, pp. 158–59.

1977

Goldberger, Paul. "Preservation Drive for a Modern Building." *New York Times,* June 8, 1977.

1978

"Grant Given for Acquisition of Schindler House." *Los Angeles Times,* December 31, 1978.

Hines, Thomas S. "Conserving the Visible Past: The Schindler House and the Los Angeles Preservation Movement." *L.A. Architect* (September 1978): n.p.

1979

"Grant Will Help in Restoring Schindler House." *Los Angeles Times,* November 25, 1979.

"Lectures, Tour Set to Benefit Schindler House." *Los Angeles Times,* May 6, 1979.

1980

"Coverage of Preservation Efforts." *Los Angeles Times,* February 17, 1980.

"Friends Acquire Schindler House." *L.A. Architect* (December 1980): n.p.

Ryon, Ruth. "Group Saves House Designed as Social Experiment." *Los Angeles Times,* July 6, 1980.

"Schindler House Celebration Slated." *Los Angeles Times,* October 19, 1980.

1981

Koeper, Frederick. "Schindler and Neutra." In Marcus Whiffen and Frederick Koeper, *American Architecture 1607–1976.* Cambridge, Mass.: The MIT Press, 1981, 334–35.

1982

"Conservancy Group Names Six Winners." *Los Angeles Times,* May 9, 1982.

"Conservancy to Present Six Preservation Awards." *Los Angeles Times,* May 30, 1982.

Dollens, Dennis. "Interview: Robert Sweeney, Executive Director of the Schindler House." *SITES* (New York) 6 (1982): 10–16.

Hines, Thomas S. *Richard Neutra and the Search for Modern Architecture: A Biography and History.* New York and Oxford: Oxford University Press, 1982, 56–58.

1983

Curtis, William J. R. *Modern Architecture since 1900.* Englewood Cliffs, N.J.: Prentice-Hall, 1983, 154–55. Second edition: 1987. Third edition: New York: Phaidon Press, 1996, 232–34.

Rollins, Bill. "Schindler House." *Los Angeles Times,* March 13, 1983.

1985

Giella, Barbara. "R. M. Schindler's Thirties Style: Its Character (1931–1937) and International Sources (1906–1937)." PhD diss., New York University. Ann Arbor, Mich.: UMI Dissertation Services, 1985, 317–19, figs. 298–304.

Kovatsch, Manfred. "Haus Schindler 1921/22: Los Angeles." In *Rudolf M. Schindler Architekt 1887–1953. Katalog zur Ausstellung Museum Villa Stuck, München, 22. November 1985—19. Januar 1986,* 24–29. Munich: Museum Villa Stuck, 1985.

1986

Neutra, Dione. *Richard Neutra, Promise and Fulfillment, 1919–1932: Selections from the Letters and Diaries of Richard and Dione Neutra,* compiled and translated by Dione Neutra. Carbondale and Edwardsville: Southern Illinois University Press, 1986, 133–80.

Sarnitz, August. *R. M. Schindler, Architect: 1887–1953.* Vienna: Akademie der bildenden Künste; Vienna and Munich: Edition Christian Brandstätter, 1986, 17, 44–47, 150–51. English edition: New York: Rizzoli, 1988.

1987

Giovannini, Joseph. "A Modernist Architect's Home Is Restored in Los Angeles." *New York Times,* December 3, 1987.

Goldberger, Paul. "A House of the Future, Now Part of Our Past." *New York Times,* December 13, 1987.

Smith, Kathryn. *R. M. Schindler House: 1921–22,* foreword by Robert L. Sweeney. West Hollywood, Calif.: Friends of the Schindler House, 1987.

1988

Sheine, Judith. "Schindler Reassessed." *Architectural Record* (New York) 176, no. 10 (September 1988): 69, 71.

1989

McCoy, Esther. "Second Guessing Schindler." *Progressive Architecture* 70, no. 4 (April 1989): 86–88.

Sweeney, Robert L. "A Real California Scheme." In *GA Houses 26.* Tokyo: A.D.A. Edita, 1989, 6–27.

1990

Ford, Edward R. "Residential Construction in America: Rudolf Schindler, Walter Gropius, and Marcel Breuer." In his *The Details of Modern Architecture.* Cambridge, Mass., and London: The MIT Press, 1990, 289–94.

Polyzoides, Stefanos. "The Schindler-Chace Duplex and Architecture." In *Concrete in California.* Los Angeles: Carpenters/Contractors Committee of Southern California, in conjunction with the School of Architecture at the University of Southern California, 1990, 30–32.

1993

Gebhard, David. "Kings Road House (R. M. Schindler and Clyde Chase *[sic]*)." In David Gebhard, ed., *The Architectural Drawings of R. M. Schindler.* New York and London: Garland Publishing, 1993, vol. 2, 370–79.

Smith, Kathryn. "The Schindler House." In *R. M. Schindler: Composition and Construction,* edited by Lionel March and Judith Sheine. London: Academy Editions, 1993, 114–23.

1994

Lacher, Irene. "Rescuing a Design Icon." *Los Angeles Times,* August 18, 1994.

Webb, Michael . "R. M. Schindler." In *Architects House Themselves: Breaking New Ground,* foreword by J. Carter Brown. Washington, D.C.: The Preservation Press/National Trust for Historic Preservation, 1994, 13–18.

1995

Boeckl, Matthias, ed. *Visionäre & Vertriebene. Österreichische Spuren in der modernen amerikasischen Architektur.* Berlin: Ernst & Sohn, 1995, 100–102, 121–22.

Frampton, Kenneth. "Rudolph Schindler, Schindler-Chase *[sic]* House, 1921–1922." In *American Masterworks: The Twentieth Century House,* edited by Kenneth Frampton and David Larkin. New York: Rizzoli, 1995, 29–33. New edition: *American Masterworks: Houses of the 20th and 21st Centuries.* New York: Rizzoli, 2008, 37–41.

Street-Porter, Tim. "The King's *[sic]* Road House by Rudolph Schindler." In *The Los Angeles House: Decoration and Design in America's 20th-Century City.* New York: Clarkson Potter, 1995, 102–5.

Sweeney, Robert L. "His House, Her House, Their House." In *MAK Center for Art and Architecture, R. M. Schindler,* edited by Peter Noever for MAK, Vienna, and MAK Center for Art and Architecture, Los Angeles. Munich and New York: Prestel, 1995, 37–49.

1996

Boehm, Bill, Daniel Johnson, and Julia Nugent. "Schindler-Chase *[sic]*. West Hollywood, 1921–22." In *Schindler and the Small House.* Boston: Boston Architectural Research Center, 1996, 28–33.

Kurrent, Friedrich. *Raummodelle: Wohnhäuser des 20. Jahrhunderts.* Salzburg and Munich: Verlag Anton Pustet, 1996, 276–77.

Noever, Peter, and William Mohline. *Zugmann: Schindler.* Santa Monica, Calif.: Form Zero Editions, 1996, front., 12–19, 21.

1997

Sweeney, Robert L. "Furnishing Kings Road: A Background for Human Activity." In *The Furniture of R. M. Schindler,* edited by Marla C. Berns. Santa Barbara: University Art Museum, University of California; Seattle and London: University of Washington Press, 1997, 58–63.

1998

Sheine, Judith. *R. M. Schindler: Works and Projects.* Barcelona: Editorial Gustavo Gili, 1998, 58–61. Chinese edition: Beijing: Liaoning Science and Technology Publishing, 2005.

Sheine, Judith, ed. "Casa Schindler-Chace, West Hollywood, California/Schindler-Chace House, West Hollywood, CA." In "R. M. Schindler, 10 Houses," *2G Revista Internacional de Arquitectura/International Architecture Review* 7, no. 3 (1998): 36–47.

1999

LeClerc, David. "R. M. Schindler: 13 Selected Works." *Kenchiku Bunka* 54, no. 635 (September 1999): 22–31 and cover.

March, Lionel. *Rudolph M. Schindler: R. M. Schindler House, Hollywood, California, 1921–22; James E. How House, Los Angeles, California, 1925.* Tokyo: A.D.A. Edita, 1999.

Sheine, Judith, ed. "R. M. Schindler: 4 Houses." *Planet Architecture* CD, vol. 3. Los Angeles: In-D Press, 1999.

2000

Pool, Bob. "Compromise Reached on Schindler House." *Los Angeles Times*, January 20, 2000.

2001

Sheine, Judith. *R. M. Schindler.* New York and London: Phaidon, 2001, 107–14.

Smith, Kathryn. *R. M. Schindler House,* new photography by Grant Mudford. New York: Harry N. Abrams, 2001; reprint, Santa Monica, Calif.: Hennessey and Ingalls, 2010.

Sweeney, Robert. "Life at Kings Road: As It Was, 1920–1940." In *The Architecture of R. M. Schindler,* edited by Elizabeth A. T. Smith and Michael Darling. Los Angeles: Museum of Contemporary Art, and New York: Harry N. Abrams, 2001, 86–115. Also published in German as "Realität in der Kings Road 1920–1940," in *R. M. Schindler Bauten und Projekte.* Ostfildern-Ruit, Germany: Hatje Cantz Verlag, 2001, and in *R. M. Schindler Architektur und Experiment.* Ostfildern-Ruit, Germany: Hatje Cantz Verlag, 2001. *See also* 2005.

Weinraub, Bernard. "Breezy Modernist Gets His Due." *New York Times,* February 26, 2001.

2003

Botnick, Marie, Pamela Burton, and Kathryn Smith. *Private Landscapes: Modernist Gardens in Southern California.* New York: Princeton Architectural Press, 2003, 18–21.

2004

Coll-Barreu, Juan. *Construcción de los paisajes inventados: Los Ángeles doméstico 1900–1960.* Barcelona: Fundación Caja de Arquitectos, 2004, 76–115.

Sheine, Judith. "R. M. Schindler y la reintegración radical del espacio interior y exterior." *Revista de Arquitectura* (Universidad de Navarra, Pamplona, Spain) 6 (June 2004): 31–42, 89–93.

2005

"Kings Road House, West Hollywood." In *Entrez lentement.* Milan: Editoriale Lotus, 2005, 98–111. Excerpted from *The Architecture of R. M. Schindler,* edited by Elizabeth A. T. Smith and Michael Darling. Los Angeles: Museum of Contemporary Art, and New York: Harry N. Abrams, 2001.

Sweeney, Robert. "The Spirit of Schindler's Kings Road House: Timeline 1921–1994." In *Schindler by MAK,* edited by Peter Noever. Munich, London, and New York: Prestel Verlag, 2005, 8–29.

———. "La vita a Kings Road: I primi anni./Life at Kings Road: The Early Years." In *Entrez lentement.* Milan: Editoriale Lotus, 2005: 112–15. Excerpted from *The Architecture of R. M. Schindler,* edited by Elizabeth A. T. Smith and Michael Darling. Los Angeles: Museum of Contemporary Art, and New York: Harry N. Abrams, 2001.

2006

Sheine, Judith. "Preserving Schindler." *arcCA* (AIACC, Sacramento, Calif.) 6, no. 3 (2006): 36–39.

2007

Bricker, Lauren, Judith Sheine, and Timothy Sakamoto. *VDL Research House.* DVD. Los Angeles: In-D Press, 2007.

2008

Lapuerta, José María de. "Casa Schindler, Los Angeles." In *Casas de Maestros.* Madrid: Arquitectura Viva SL, 2008, 4–15.

Mitchell, Sean. "Their All-Time Favorite Houses." *Los Angeles Times,* December 27, 2008, Home section. Identifies Schindler's Kings Road house as number 1 in a survey of architects, preservationists, and academics.

Sheine, Judith. "Wide Open Spaces." *Art and Antiques* 31, no. 9 (September 2008): 86–92.

2009

Sheine, Judith. "R. M. Schindler." In *Oxford Companion to Architecture,* edited by Patrick Goode. Oxford: Oxford University Press, 2009, 809–10.

2010

Browning, Dominique, and Lucy Gilmour. "Schindler House." In *Living Architecture: Greatest American Houses of the 20th Century.* New York: Assouline, 2010, 106–17.

Hines, Thomas S. *Architecture of the Sun: Los Angeles Modernism 1900–1970.* New York: Rizzoli, 2010, 239–46.

INDEX

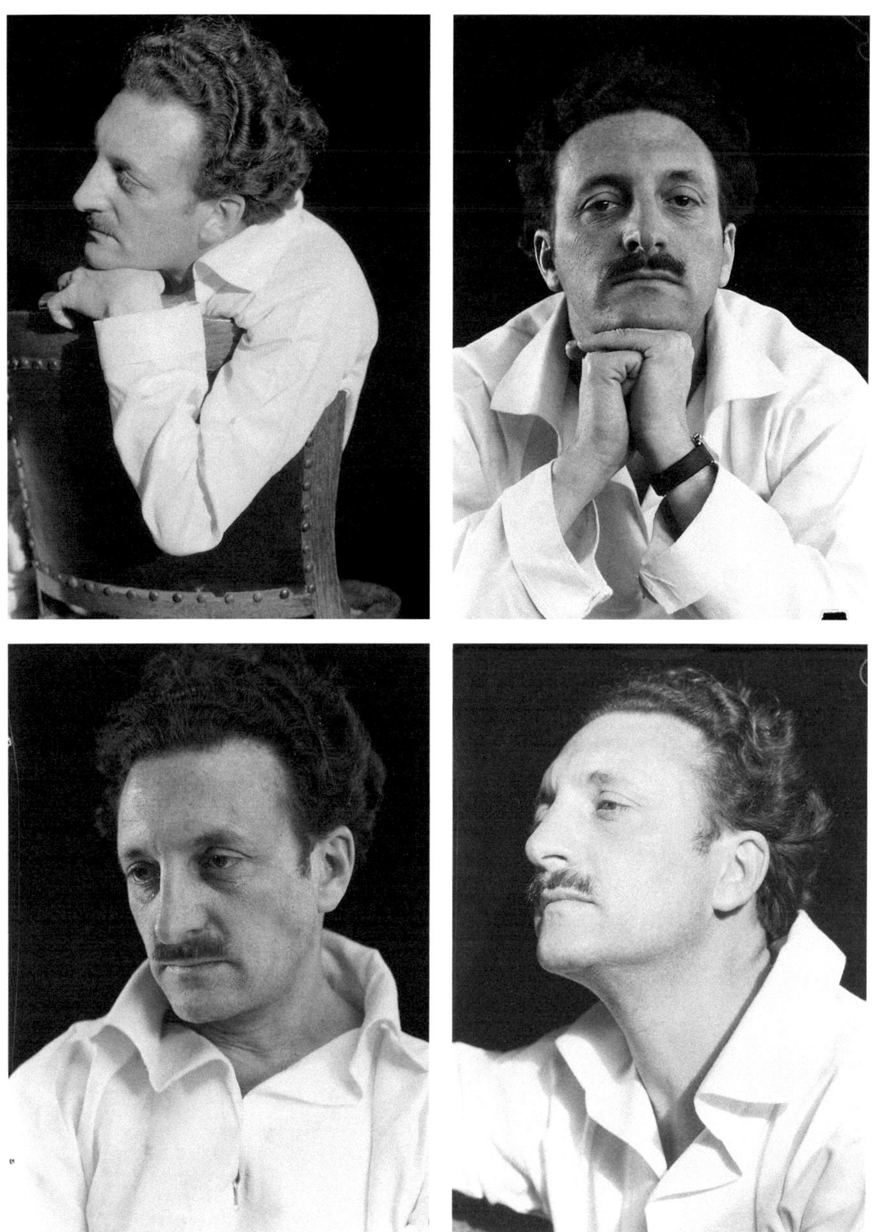

Photographs by Edward Weston, untitled [Rudolph Schindler], circa 1927. Posthumous digital reproductions from original negatives, Edward Weston Archive, Center for Creative Photography,

DESIGNER AND COMPOSITOR CLAUDIA SMELSER

TEXT MONOTYPE BULMER

DISPLAY FUTURA BOOK

PREPRESS IOCOLOR